Plant Based Cookbook for Women 2021

600-Day Essential Plant Based Recipes to Increase Energy and Balance Hormones

Miegan Darkey

© Copyright 2021 Miegan Darkey - All Rights Reserved.

In no way is it legal to reproduce, duplicate, or transmit any part of this document by either electronic means or in printed format. Recording of this publication is strictly prohibited, and any storage of this material is not allowed unless with written permission from the publisher. All rights reserved.

The information provided herein is stated to be truthful and consistent, in that any liability, regarding inattention or otherwise, by any usage or abuse of any policies, processes, or directions contained within is the solitary and complete responsibility of the recipient reader. Under no circumstances will any legal liability or blame be held against the publisher for any reparation, damages, or monetary loss due to the information herein, either directly or indirectly.

Respective authors own all copyrights not held by the publisher.

Legal Notice:

This book is copyright protected. This is only for personal use. You cannot amend, distribute, sell, use, quote or paraphrase any part of the content within this book without the consent of the author or copyright owner. Legal action will be pursued if this is breached.

Disclaimer Notice:

Please note the information contained within this document is for educational and entertainment purposes only. Every attempt has been made to provide accurate, up-to-date and reliable, complete information. No warranties of any kind are expressed or implied. Readers acknowledge that the author is not engaging in the rendering of legal, financial, medical or professional advice.

By reading this document, the reader agrees that under no circumstances are we responsible for any losses, direct or indirect, which are incurred as a result of the use of information contained within this document, including, but not limited to, errors, omissions, or inaccuracies.

Table of contents

Introduction 6
Chapter 1: Understanding the Plant-Based Diet 7
    What is Plant-Based Diet? 7
    Benefits of Plant-Based Diet 7
    How do You Start a Plant-Based Diet? 9
    What to Eat and Avoid on a Plant-Based Diet? 10
Chapter 2: Breakfast 11

Spiced Strawberry Smoothie 11	Vegan Fried Egg 16
Peanut Butter and Banana Bread Granola 12	Blueberry Muffins 17
	Ultimate Breakfast Sandwich 18
Scrambled Eggs with Aquafaba 13	Chickpea Omelet 19
Fig Oatmeal Bake 14	Pancake 20
Vegan Breakfast Sandwich 15	

Chapter 3: Soups and Stews 21

Wonton Soup 21	Curry Lentil Soup 30
Butternut Squash and Coconut Milk Soup 22	Cream of Mushroom Soup 31
	Spinach and Cannellini Bean Stew 32
Vegan Pho..................................... 23	
Root Vegetable Stew 24	Red Pepper and Tomato Soup 33
Portobello Mushroom Stew........... 25	Broccoli Cheese Soup 34
Sweet Potato, Kale and Peanut Stew 26	Cauliflower and Horseradish Soup 35
Spicy Bean Stew 27	Black Bean and Quinoa Stew 36
Brussel Sprouts Stew 28	Kimchi Stew 37
Mexican Lentil Soup 29	Fennel and Chickpeas Provençal .. 38

Chapter 4: Salads 39

Cranberry and Quinoa Salad 39	Butternut Squash Quinoa Salad ... 46
Zucchini Salad 40	Butternut Squash and Kale Salad . 47
Grilled Corn Salad Bowl 41	Vegan Caesar Salad 48
Pear, Pomegranate and Roasted Butternut Squash Salad 42	Tropical Radicchio Slaw................ 49
	Heirloom Tomato Salad................ 50
Greens Salad with Black Eyed Peas 43	Spiralized Zucchini and Carrot Salad 51
Chopped Kale Power Salad 44	Lemon, Basil and Orzo Salad 52
Kale Slaw....................................... 45	Kohlrabi Slaw 53

Chapter 5: Beans and Grains 54

Stuffed Peppers 54
Quinoa and Black Bean Chili 55
Sweet Potato and White Bean Skillet 56
Zucchini Risotto 57
Black Beans and Rice 58
Falafel 59
Zoodles with White Beans 60
Lentil and Chickpea Salad 61
Rice Stuffed Jalapeños 62
Quinoa Meatballs 63
Tomato, Kale, and White Bean Skillet 64
Chickpea Fajitas 65
Mexican Stuffed Peppers 66
Lentil, Rice and Vegetable Bake ... 67
Mediterranean Chickpea Casserole 68
Black Bean Stuffed Sweet Potatoes 69

Chapter 6: Vegetables 70
Pesto with Squash Ribbons and Fettuccine 70
Grilled Asparagus and Shiitake Tacos 71
Thai Tofu 72
Middle Eastern Salad Tacos 73
Stuffed Peppers with Kidney Beans 74
Thai Peanut Sauce over Roasted Sweet Potatoes 75
Beans Curry 76
Ratatouille 77
Summer Minestrone 78
Mushroom and Broccoli Noodles . 79
Balsamic-Glazed Roasted Cauliflower 80
Pasta with Creamy Greens and Lemon 81
Blackened Tempeh 82
Avocado Linguine 83
Tomato and Basil Sauce 84
Zaatar Roasted Eggplant 85
Butternut Squash Linguine 86
Vegetarian fajitas 87
Spiced Carrot and Lentil Soup 88

Chapter 7: Snack and Sides 89
Zucchini Chips 89
Pumpkin Cake Pops 90
Cinnamon Bananas 91
Oven-Dried Grapes 92
Beans and Spinach Tacos 93
Black Bean Lime Dip 94
Watermelon Pizza 95
Zucchini and Amaranth Patties 96
Rice Pizza 97
Applesauce 98
Quinoa and Black Bean Burgers ... 99
Loaded Baked Potatoes 100

Chapter 8: Desserts 101
Cookie Dough Bites 101
Coconut Lemon Tart 102
Strawberry Coconut Ice Cream ... 103
Chocolate and Avocado Truffles . 104
Chocolate Avocado Ice Cream 105
Chocolate Peanut Butter Energy Bites 106
Dark Chocolate Raspberry Ice Cream 107
Strawberry Mousse 108
Brownie Batter 109

Peanut Butter Energy Bars 110
Mango Coconut Cheesecake 111
Chocolate Mint Grasshopper Pie 112
Lemon Cashew Tart 113
Matcha Coconut Cream Pie 114

Chapter 9: Homemade Basics, Sauces, and Condiments 115
Tomato Jam 115
Green Goddess Hummus 116
Barbecue Tahini Sauce 117
Spicy Red Wine Tomato Sauce ... 118
Garlic Alfredo Sauce 119
Cilantro and Parsley Hot Sauce .. 120
Kale and Walnut Pesto 121
Cashew Yogurt 122
Nacho Cheese Sauce 123
Thai Peanut Sauce 124
Garden Pesto 125
Buffalo Chicken Dip 126
Hot Sauce 127
Alfredo Sauce 128

Chapter 10: Drinks 129
Mango Lassi 129
Chard, Lettuce and Ginger Smoothie 130
Green Lemonade 131
Banana Milk 132
Strawberry and Hemp Smoothie . 133
Pumpkin Spice Frappuccino 134
Turmeric Lassi 135
Red Beet, Pear and Apple Smoothie 136
Banana and Protein Smoothie 137
Hazelnut and Chocolate Milk 138
Berry and Yogurt Smoothie 139
Fruit Infused Water 140
Spiced Buttermilk 141
Strawberry and Pineapple Smoothie 142

Conclusion 143

Introduction

Modern cutting-edge nutritional research has clearly identified the whole food plant-based diet as the single most potent force for recovering and sustaining human health. Only a diet rich in a wide variety of fresh fruits, vegetables, beans, mushrooms, nuts, berries, and seeds—and which is free of highly processed foods, laden with preservatives, refined oils, sugar, and salt—has the power to reverse many of the leading chronic diseases the world faces today, including heart disease, diabetes, obesity, high blood, autoimmune disorders, and more.

With this Plant Based cookbook as your ultimate guide, it has never been easier to make the life-changing switch to a plant-based diet. Soon to become an essential cookbook in healthy kitchens around the world, the Plant Based Cookbook is your key to finally finding your own path to better health.

Chapter 1: Understanding the Plant-Based Diet

What is Plant-Based Diet?

This diet means to mostly consume plant-derived food products such as greens, grains, fruits, and nuts. The individual can choose the level of restrictions on meat and other products. Being a vegan is not the only way to become someone who eats a plant-based diet. There are several types:

- **Flexitarian**

Those that follow this diet do not completely cut off any type of food. They can eat dairy, meat, and seafood. It's according to the person's needs

- **Pescatarian**

As the name suggests, in this diet along with plants, seafood and eggs can be eaten without hesitation.

- **Vegetarian**

Those that eat eggs and other dairy products with plant-based foods. They cannot eat fish or any meat.

- **Vegan**

They are strict plant-based food eaters who eat nothing in their diet but plant-derived foods.

Plants can provide high nutrients filled with protein and fat and lots of fiber but it lacks a few minerals and vitamins. To compensate for them, store-bought supplements need to be added to the diet.

Benefits of Plant-Based Diet

There are many benefits to follow this diet mainly overall increase in wellness and being less sick. The concept has been around for a long time that increasing consumption of plant-derived foods makes the person more active and healthier. These people also seem to be happier and less irritated which makes life easier and far more relaxing. There are other advantages which comes with the diet. Some of them are listed below:

- There's no need to count calories in this diet. It can be a tedious and time-wasting task that a busy person cannot afford. This diet simply allows some food and restricts the rest. A calorie doesn't tell much about the food, what nutrients are in it or is it healthy or not.
- It is a good way to lose weight. A recent 2018 control experiment showed that people that follow a vegan diet rather than those who eat meat, were more likely to lose weight. The study followed obese participants following there normal and some following vegan diets and the result was that dieters almost lost 15 pounds in 4 months.
- Plant-based foods are full of carbs and fiber which fills up the stomach quickly making you feel less hungry. You will consume less of the foods that will be no good for you like sodas or candies. Cravings will not hit you as hard as if you were hungry.
- There is a higher quantity of water in plant-based food which increases body metabolism and reduces appetite. Water has many benefits, being hydrated makes you have better hair, skin and makes you look fresh.
- Eating mostly plant-based foods increases mortality by preventing life long diseases. A recent 2019 done by the American Heart Association showed that plant-eaters were less likely to develop heart diseases. It is also linked with lowering the chances of stroke, diabetes type 2, hypertension, and obesity.
- It also has shown to increase insulin sensitivity in diabetic patients. In the 2009 study, over tens of thousands of participants were approached and the percentage of vegans developing diabetes was found to be 2.9% less than others. A review published in 2018 stated that diabetes is improved when following any diet that increases plant content.
- By following this diet, you will not only help yourself in becoming better but also push the environment to progress in the right direction. A lot of pollutants come from Barnes and poultry farms. Making meat puts high stress on our planet and by consuming less of it, you are leaving less of a carbon footprint. Also, by this diet, you are discouraging the use of meat as well.
- It doesn't require any sort of investment and a person can begin it as soon as they decide to. Plant-based products are everywhere and even in a normal diet, take a big portion of it. Some dieting programs and fads take a lot of money from people giving only temporary results but this diet has shown to reduce the most amount of weight.

For some people starting this diet can be hard but if you want to reach your weight loss goals or become generally more fit than this diet is suited for you.

How do You Start a Plant-Based Diet?

There are a few lifestyle changes one needs to do to start a plant-based diet. Going in too strongly will cause tension to build up only to be blown when a craving hit. Some may find it very difficult to follow but you only need to keep a few points in mind to achieve success.

- Increase greens in your diet. A variety of vegetables are present for choosing to offer different flavors and textures for soothing your tongue. Pick vegetables regularly for meal bases and a replacement for unhealthy snacks. The crunchiness and flavors of some veggies might decrease the likelihood of eating junk food.
- Most healthy diets don't just forbid the consumption of fats but instead tells you to replace bad fats which are derived from animals with good ones derived from plants. Seeds and olive oil are a good source of healthy fats which do not increase the body cholesterol levels.
- Cut down meat, especially red meat as much as you can. You can still consume it if you are following a more lenient diet but it is discouraged. Replace your meat with seafood or tofu which can be a good substitute for it.
- Rather than putting desserts on the table, you should place fruits or fruit dishes. They are a healthier option with the same hints of sugar to satisfy the sweet tooth. Some people crave sugar more, they can slowly cut off sugar from their diet by switching it for sweet fruits instead.
- Replace everyday cow's milk for plant-derived milk such as soy, almond, rice or coconut. Milk is an important part of a diet that is impractical to fully remove from the diet.
- Stay away from foods that have a lot of sugar like a Pepsi or are high in fat like french fries. Also do not buy processed food because they are riddled with salt and sugar, which are enemies to your body.
- Be aware that not every nutrient is being provided fully and arrange a replacement for that. Vit B12 is present in some cereal and in nutritional yeast. Iron is also less consumed so eat a healthy dose of cabbage, spinach or kidney beans to make up for it.

What to Eat and Avoid on a Plant-Based Diet?

You can eat:

- All vegetables, including greens like spinach, kale, chards, collards, asparagus, broccoli, cauliflower, bell peppers, tomatoes, onion, etc
- All fruits, including berries, avocado, apple, banana, watermelon, grapes, oranges, etc
- Plant-based alternates to meat like tofu and tempeh
- Plant-based milk and dairy products including coconut milk, almond milk, peanut butter, almond butter, cashew yogurt, etc
- All whole-grains, including brown rice, amaranth, quinoa, barley, all beans, whole wheat pasta, whole-grain bread, etc
- All nuts, including cashews, almonds, walnuts, macadamia nuts, etc
- All seeds like chia seeds, flaxseed, hempseeds, etc
- Lentils
- Millets
- Flax eggs
- Honey, maple syrup, coconut sugar, stevia, Splenda, erythritol, etc
- Unsweetened coffee and tea

You can not eat:

- Meat including beef, pork, and poultry
- Seafood including fish and shrimps
- Processed animal products like hot dogs, sausages
- Dairy items like butter, eggs, whole milk, yogurt, etc
- Sweetened drinks like soda, fruit juices, sweetened tea and coffee
- Fried food and fast foods
- White bread and white pasta

Chapter 2: Breakfast

Spiced Strawberry Smoothie

Preparation time: 5 minutes
Cooking time: 0 minute
Servings: 1

Ingredients:

- 1 tablespoon goji berries, soaked
- 1 cup strawberries
- 1/8 teaspoon sea salt
- 1 frozen banana
- 1 Medjool date, pitted
- 1 scoop vanilla-flavored whey protein
- 2 tablespoons lemon juice
- ¼ teaspoon ground ginger
- ½ teaspoon ground cinnamon
- 1 tablespoon almond butter
- 1 cup almond milk, unsweetened

Method:

1. Place all the ingredients in the order in a food processor or blender and then pulse for 2 to 3 minutes at high speed until smooth.
2. Pour the smoothie into a glass and then serve.

Nutrition Value:

- Calories: 182 Cal
- Fat: 1.3 g
- Carbs: 34 g
- Protein: 6.4 g
- Fiber: 0.7 g

Peanut Butter and Banana Bread Granola

Preparation time: 10 minutes
Cooking time: 32 minutes
Servings: 6

Ingredients:

- 1/2 cup Quinoa
- 1/2 cup mashed banana
- 3 cup rolled oats, old-fashioned
- 1 cup banana chips, crushed
- 1 cup peanuts, salted
- 1 teaspoon. salt
- 1 teaspoon. cinnamon
- 1/4 cup brown sugar
- 1/4 cup honey
- 2 teaspoon. vanilla extract, unsweetened
- 1/3 cup peanut butter
- 6 tablespoon. unsalted butter

Method:

1. Switch on the oven, then set it to 325 degrees F and let it preheat.
2. Meanwhile, take two rimmed baking sheets, line them with parchment sheets, and set aside until required.
3. Place oats in a bowl, add quinoa, banana chips, cinnamon, salt, and sugar and stir until combined.
4. Take a small saucepan, place it over medium-low heat, add butter and honey and cook for 4 minutes until melted, stirring frequently.
5. Then remove the pan from heat, add banana and vanilla, stir until mixed, then spoon the mixture into the oat mixture and stir until incorporated.
6. Distribute granola evenly between two baking sheets, spread evenly, and then bake for 25 minutes until golden brown, rotating the sheets halfway.
7. When done, transfer baking sheets on wire racks, cool the granola, then break it into pieces and serve.
8. Serve straight away.

Nutrition Value:

- Calories: 655 Cal
- Fat: 36 g
- Carbs: 70 g
- Protein: 18 g
- Fiber: 12 g

Scrambled Eggs with Aquafaba

Preparation time: 5 minutes
Cooking time: 15 minutes
Servings: 2

Ingredients:

- 6 ounces tofu, firm, pressed, drained
- 1/2 cup aquafaba
- 1 1/2 tablespoons olive oil
- 1 tablespoon nutritional yeast
- 1/4 teaspoon black salt
- 1/8 teaspoon ground turmeric
- 1/4 teaspoon ground black pepper

Method:

1. Take a food processor, add tofu, yeast, black pepper, salt, and turmeric, then pour in aquafaba and olive oil and pulse for 1 minute until smooth.
2. Take a skillet pan, place it over medium heat, and when hot, add tofu mixture and cook for 1 minute.
3. Cover the pan, continue cooking for 3 minutes, then uncover the pan and pull the mixture across the pan with a wooden spoon until soft forms.
4. Continue cooking for 10 minutes until resembles soft scrambled eggs, folding tofu mixture gently and heat over medium heat, then remove the pan from heat and season with salt and black pepper to taste.
5. Serve straight away

Nutrition Value:

- Calories: 208 Cal
- Fat: 5.1 g
- Carbs: 31.3 g
- Protein: 8.3 g
- Fiber: 10.4 g

Fig Oatmeal Bake

Preparation time: 5 minutes
Cooking time: 15 minutes
Servings: 4

Ingredients:

- 2 fresh figs, sliced
- 5 dried figs, chopped
- 4 tablespoons chopped walnuts
- 1 ½ cups oats
- 1 teaspoon cinnamon
- 2 tablespoons agave syrup
- 1 teaspoon baking powder
- 2 tablespoons unsalted butter, melted
- 3 tablespoons flaxseed egg
- ¾ cup of coconut milk

Method:

1. Switch on the oven, then set it to 350 degrees F and let it preheat.
2. Meanwhile, take a bowl, place all the ingredients in it, except for fresh figs and stir until combined.
3. Take an 8-inch square pan, line it with parchment sheet, spoon in the prepared mixture, top with fig slices, and bake for 30 minutes until cooked and set.
4. Serve straight away

Nutrition Value:

- Calories: 372.8 Cal
- Fat: 9.2 g
- Carbs: 65.6 g
- Protein: 11.6 g
- Fiber: 11.1 g

Vegan Breakfast Sandwich

Preparation time: 15 minutes
Cooking time: 8 minutes
Servings: 3

Ingredients:
- 1 cup of spinach
- 6 slices of pickle
- 14 oz tofu, extra-firm, pressed
- 2 medium tomatoes, sliced
- 1/2 teaspoon garlic powder
- ¼ teaspoon ground black pepper
- 1/2 teaspoon black salt
- 1 teaspoon turmeric
- 1 tablespoon coconut oil
- 2 tablespoons vegan mayo
- 3 slices of vegan cheese
- 6 slices of gluten-free bread, toasted

Method:
1. Cut tofu into six slices, and then season its one side with garlic, black pepper, salt, and turmeric.
2. Take a skillet pan, place it over medium heat, add oil and when hot, add seasoned tofu slices in it, season side down, and cook for 3 minutes until crispy and light brown.
3. Then flip the tofu slices and continue cooking for 3 minutes until browned and crispy.
4. When done, transfer tofu slices on a baking sheet, in the form of a set of two slices side by side, then top each set with a cheese slice and broil for 3 minutes until cheese has melted.
5. Spread mayonnaise on both sides of slices, top with two slices of tofu, cheese on the side, top with spinach, tomatoes, pickles, and then close the sandwich.
6. Cut the sandwich into half and then serve.

Nutrition Value:
- Calories: 364 Cal
- Fat: 12 g
- Carbs: 51 g
- Protein: 16 g
- Fiber: 3 g

Vegan Fried Egg

Preparation time: 5 minutes
Cooking time: 8 minutes
Servings: 4

Ingredients:

- 1 block of firm tofu, firm, pressed, drained
- ½ teaspoon ground black pepper
- ½ teaspoon salt
- 1 tablespoon vegan butter
- 1 cup vegan toast dipping sauce

Method:

1. Cut tofu into four slices, and then shape them into a rough circle by using a cookie cutter.
2. Take a frying pan, place it over medium heat, add butter and when it melts, add prepared tofu slices in a single layer and cook for 3 minutes per side until light brown.
3. Transfer tofu to serving dishes, make a small hole in the middle of tofu by using a small cookie cutter and fill the hole with dipping sauce.
4. Garnish eggs with black pepper and sauce and then serve.

Nutrition Value:

- Calories: 86 Cal
- Fat: 9 g
- Carbs: 0.5 g
- Protein: 2 g
- Fiber: 0 g

Blueberry Muffins

Preparation time: 5 minutes
Cooking time: 15 minutes
Servings: 12

Ingredients:

- 2 cups fresh blueberries
- 2 cups all-purpose flour
- 2½ teaspoons baking powder
- ½ teaspoon salt
- ¼ teaspoon baking soda
- ½ cup and 2 tablespoon. sugar
- zest of 1 lemon
- 1 teaspoon apple cider vinegar
- ¼ cup and 2 tablespoons. canola oil
- 1 cup of soy milk
- 1 teaspoon vanilla extract, unsweetened

Method:

1. Switch on the oven, then set it to 450 degrees F and let it preheat.
2. Meanwhile, take a small bowl, add vinegar and milk, whisk until combined, and let it stand to curdle.
3. Take a large bowl, add flour, salt, baking powder, and soda, and stir until mixed.
4. Whisk in sugar, lemon zest, oil, and vanilla into soy milk mixture, then gradually whisk in flour mixture until incorporated and fold in berries until combined.
5. Take a twelve cups muffin tray, grease them with oil, distribute the prepared batter in them and bake for 25 minutes until done and the tops are browned.
6. Let muffins cool for 5 minutes, then cool them completely and serve.

Nutrition Value:

- Calories: 160 Cal
- Fat: 5 g
- Carbs: 25 g
- Protein: 2 g
- Fiber: 2 g

Ultimate Breakfast Sandwich

Preparation time: 40 minutes
 Cooking time: 10 minutes
 Servings: 4

Ingredients:

For the Tofu:
- 12 ounces tofu, extra-firm, pressed, drain
- 1/2 teaspoon garlic powder
- 1 teaspoon liquid smoke
- 2 tablespoons nutritional yeast
- 1 teaspoon Sriracha sauce
- 2 tablespoons soy sauce
- 2 tablespoons olive oil
- 2 tablespoons water

For the Vegan Breakfast Sandwich:
- 1 large tomato, sliced
- 4 English muffins, halved, toasted
- 1 avocado, mashed

Method:

1. Prepare tofu, and for this, cut tofu into four slices and set aside.
2. Stir together remaining ingredients of tofu, pour the mixture into a bag, then add tofu pieces, toss until coated and marinate for 30 minutes.
3. Take a skillet pan, place it over medium-high heat, add tofu slices along with the marinade and cook for 5 minutes per side.
4. Prepare sandwich and for this, spread mashed avocado on the inner of the muffin, top with a slice of tofu, layer with a tomato slice and then serve.

Nutrition Value:
- Calories: 277 Cal
- Fat: 9.1 g
- Carbs: 33.1 g
- Protein: 16.1 g
- Fiber: 3.6 g

Chickpea Omelet

Preparation time: 5 minutes
Cooking time: 10 minutes
Servings: 1

Ingredients:

- 3 Tablespoon chickpea flour
- 1 small white onion, peeled, diced
- ½ teaspoon black salt
- 2 tablespoons chopped the dill
- 2 tablespoons chopped basil
- 1/8 teaspoon ground black pepper
- 2 Tablespoon olive oil
- 8 Tablespoon water

Method:

1. Take a bowl, add flour in it along with salt and black pepper, stir until mixed, and then whisk in water until creamy.
2. Take a skillet pan, place it over medium heat, add 1 tablespoon oil and when hot, add onion and cook for 4 minutes until cooked.
3. Add onion to omelet mixture and then stir until combined.
4. Add remaining oil into the pan, pour in prepared batter, spread evenly, and cook for 3 minutes per side until cooked.
5. Serve omelet with bread.

Nutrition Value:

- Calories: 150 Cal
- Fat: 2 g
- Carbs: 24.4 g
- Protein: 10.2 g
- Fiber: 5.8 g

Pancake

Preparation time: 10 minutes
Cooking time: 18 minutes
Servings: 4

Ingredients:

Dry Ingredients:
- 1 cup buckwheat flour
- 1/8 teaspoon salt
- ½ teaspoon gluten-free baking powder
- ½ teaspoon baking soda

Wet Ingredients:
- 1 tablespoon almond butter
- 2 tablespoon maple syrup
- 1 tablespoon lime juice
- 1 cup coconut milk, unsweetened

Method:
1. Take a medium bowl, add all the dry ingredients and stir until mixed.
2. Take another bowl, place all the wet ingredients, whisk until combined, and then gradually whisk in dry ingredients mixture until smooth and incorporated.
3. Take a frying pan, place it over medium heat, add 2 teaspoons oil and when hot, drop in batter and cook for 3 minutes per side until cooked and lightly browned.
4. Serve pancakes and fruits and maple syrup.

Nutrition Value:
- Calories: 148 Cal
- Fat: 8.2 g
- Carbs: 15 g
- Protein: 4.6 g
- Fiber: 1.7 g

Chapter 3: Soups and Stews

Wonton Soup

Preparation time: 15 minutes
Cooking time: 10 minutes
Servings: 4

Ingredients:

For the Soup:
- 4 cups vegetable broth
- 2 green onions, chopped

For the Wontons Filling:
- 1 cup chopped mushrooms
- 1/4 cup walnuts, chopped
- 1 green onion, chopped
- 1/2 inch of ginger, grated
- ½ teaspoon minced garlic
- 1 tablespoon rice vinegar
- 2 teaspoons soy sauce
- 1 teaspoon brown sugar
- 20 Vegan Wonton Wrappers

Method:

1. Prepare wonton filling and for this, take a bowl, place all the ingredients in it, except for wrapper and toss until well combined.
2. Place a wonton wrapper on working space, place 1 teaspoon of prepared filling in the middle, then brush some water at the edges, fold over to shape like a half-moon, and seal the wrappers by pinching the edges.
3. Take a large pot, place it over medium-high heat, add broth, and bring it to boil.
4. Then drop prepared wontons in it, one at a time, and boil for 5 minutes.
5. When cooked, garnish the soup with green onions and serve.

Nutrition Value:

- Calories: 196.9 Cal
- Fat: 4 g
- Carbs: 31 g
- Protein: 6.6 g
- Fiber: 2.4 g

Butternut Squash and Coconut Milk Soup

Preparation time: 10 minutes
Cooking time: 35 minutes
Servings: 6

Ingredients:

- 1 cup diced parsnips
- 2 cups diced sweet potato
- 1 large sweet onion, peeled, diced
- 1 ½ cups diced carrots
- 4 cups diced butternut squash
- 2 teaspoons minced garlic
- 1/4 teaspoon ground ginger
- ¼ teaspoon ground black pepper
- ½ teaspoon of sea salt
- 1/4 teaspoon ground allspice
- 1 teaspoon poultry seasoning
- 1 teaspoon pumpkin pie spice
- 1/4 teaspoon ground cinnamon
- 32 ounces vegetable stock
- 14 ounces coconut milk, unsweetened

Method:

1. Take a large Dutch oven, place it over medium heat, add onions, drizzle with 2 tablespoons water and cook for 5 minutes until softened, drizzling with more 2 tablespoons at a time if required.
2. Then stir in garlic, cook for another minute, switch heat to the high level, add remaining ingredients, reserving milk, salt, and black pepper, and bring the soup to boil.
3. Then switch heat to medium-low level and simmer for 20 minutes until vegetables are tender.
4. When done, puree soup by using an immersion blender, then stir in coconut milk, season with salt and black pepper and cook for 3 minutes until warm.
5. Serve straight away.

Nutrition Value:

- Calories: 188.4 Cal
- Fat: 7.7 g
- Carbs: 29.3 g
- Protein: 3.7 g
- Fiber: 8.2 g

Vegan Pho

Preparation time: 5 minutes
Cooking time: 15 minutes
Servings: 6

Ingredients:

- 1 package of wide rice noodles, cooked
- 1 medium white onion, peeled, quartered
- 2 teaspoons minced garlic
- 1 inch of ginger, sliced into coins
- 8 cups vegetable broth
- 3 whole cloves
- 2 tablespoons soy sauce
- 3 whole star anise
- 1 cinnamon stick
- 3 cups of water

For Toppings:

- Basil as needed for topping
- Chopped green onions as needed for topping
- Ming beans as needed for topping
- Hot sauce as needed for topping
- Lime wedges for serving

Method:

1. Take a large pot, place it over medium-high heat, add all the ingredients for soup in it, except for soy sauce and broth, and bring it to boil.
2. Then switch heat to medium-low level, simmer the soup for 30 minutes and then stir in soy sauce.
3. When done, distribute cooked noodles into bowls, top with soup, then top with toppings and serve.

Nutrition Value:

- Calories: 31 Cal
- Fat: 0 g
- Carbs: 7 g
- Protein: 0 g
- Fiber: 2 g

Root Vegetable Stew

Preparation time: 10 minutes
Cooking time: 8 hours and 10 minutes
Servings: 6

Ingredients:

- 2 cups chopped kale
- 1 large white onion, peeled, chopped
- 1 pound parsnips, peeled, chopped
- 1 pound potatoes, peeled, chopped
- 2 celery ribs, chopped
- 1 pound butternut squash, peeled, deseeded, chopped
- 1 pound carrots, peeled, chopped
- 3 teaspoons minced garlic
- 1 pound sweet potatoes, peeled, chopped
- 1 bay leaf
- 1 teaspoon ground black pepper
- 1/2 teaspoon sea salt
- 1 tablespoon chopped sage
- 3 cups vegetable broth

Method:

1. Switch on the slow cooker, add all the ingredients in it, except for the kale, and stir until mixed.
2. Shut the cooker with lid and cook for 8 hours at a low heat setting until cooked.
3. When done, add kale into the stew, stir until mixed, and cook for 10 minutes until leaves have wilted.
4. Serve straight away.

Nutrition Value:

- Calories: 120 Cal
- Fat: 1 g
- Carbs: 28 g
- Protein: 4 g
- Fiber: 6 g

Portobello Mushroom Stew

Preparation time: 10 minutes
Cooking time: 8 hours
Servings: 4

Ingredients:

- 8 cups vegetable broth
- 1 cup dried wild mushrooms
- 1 cup dried chickpeas
- 3 cups chopped potato
- 2 cups chopped carrots
- 1 cup corn kernels
- 2 cups diced white onions
- 1 tablespoon minced parsley
- 3 cups chopped zucchini
- 1 tablespoon minced rosemary
- 1 1/2 teaspoon ground black pepper
- 1 teaspoon dried sage
- 2/3 teaspoon salt
- 1 teaspoon dried oregano
- 3 tablespoons soy sauce
- 1 1/2 teaspoons liquid smoke
- 8 ounces tomato paste

Method:

1. Switch on the slow cooker, add all the ingredients in it, and stir until mixed.
2. Shut the cooker with lid and cook for 10 hours at a high heat setting until cooked.
3. Serve straight away.

Nutrition Value:

- Calories: 447 Cal
- Fat: 36 g
- Carbs: 24 g
- Protein: 11 g
- Fiber: 2 g

Sweet Potato, Kale and Peanut Stew

Preparation time: 10 minutes
Cooking time: 45 minutes
Servings: 3

Ingredients:

- 1/4 cup red lentils
- 2 medium sweet potatoes, peeled, cubed
- 1 medium white onion, peeled, diced
- 1 cup kale, chopped
- 2 tomatoes, diced
- 1/4 cup chopped green onion
- 1 teaspoon minced garlic
- 1 inch of ginger, grated
- 2 tablespoons toasted peanuts
- ¼ teaspoon ground black pepper
- 1 teaspoon ground cumin
- 1/2 teaspoon turmeric
- 1/8 teaspoon cayenne pepper
- 1 tablespoon peanut butter
- 1 1/2 cups vegetable broth
- 2 teaspoons coconut oil

Method:

1. Take a medium pot, place it medium heat, add oil and when it melts, add onions and cook for 5 minutes.
2. Then stir in ginger and garlic, cook for 2 minutes until fragrant, add lentils and potatoes along with all the spices, and stir until mixed.
3. Stir in tomatoes, pour in the broth, bring the mixture to boil, then switch heat to the low level and simmer for 30 minutes until cooked.
4. Then stir in peanut butter until incorporated and then puree by using an immersion blender until half-pureed.
5. Return stew over low heat, stir in kale, cook for 5 minutes until its leaves wilts, and then season with black pepper and salt.
6. Garnish the stew with peanuts and green onions and then serve.

Nutrition Value:

- Calories: 401 Cal
- Fat: 6.7 g
- Carbs: 77.3 g
- Protein: 10.8 g
- Fiber: 16 g

Spicy Bean Stew

Preparation time: 5 minutes
Cooking time: 50 minutes
Servings: 4

Ingredients:

- 7 ounces cooked black eye beans
- 14 ounces chopped tomatoes
- 2 medium carrots, peeled, diced
- 7 ounces cooked kidney beans
- 1 leek, diced
- ½ a chili, chopped
- 1 teaspoon minced garlic
- 1/3 teaspoon ground black pepper
- 2/3 teaspoon salt
- 1 teaspoon red chili powder
- 1 lemon, juiced
- 3 tablespoons white wine
- 1 tablespoon olive oil
- 1 2/3 cups vegetable stock

Method:

1. Take a large saucepan, place it over medium-high heat, add oil and when hot, add leeks and cook for 8 minutes or until softened.
2. Then add carrots, continue cooking for 4 minutes, stir in chili and garlic, pour in the wine, and continue cooking for 2 minutes.
3. Add tomatoes, stir in lemon juice, pour in the stock and bring the mixture to boil.
4. Switch heat to medium level, simmer for 35 minutes until stew has thickened, then add both beans along with remaining ingredients and cook for 5 minutes until hot.
5. Serve straight away.

Nutrition Value:

- Calories: 114 Cal
- Fat: 1.6 g
- Carbs: 19 g
- Protein: 6 g
- Fiber: 8.4 g

Brussel Sprouts Stew

Preparation time: 10 minutes
Cooking time: 55 minutes
Servings: 4

Ingredients:

- 35 ounces Brussels sprouts
- 5 medium potato, peeled, chopped
- 1 medium onion, peeled, chopped
- 2 carrot, peeled, cubed
- 2 teaspoons smoked paprika
- 1/8 teaspoon ground black pepper
- 1/8 teaspoon salt
- 3 tablespoons caraway seeds
- 1/2 teaspoon red chili powder
- 1 tablespoon nutmeg
- 1 tablespoon olive oil
- 4 ½ cups hot vegetable stock

Method:

1. Take a large pot, place it over medium-high heat, add oil and when hot, add onion and cook for 1 minute.
2. Then add carrot and potato, cook for 2 minutes, then add Brussel sprouts and cook for 5 minutes.
3. Stir in all the spices, pour in vegetable stock, bring the mixture to boil, switch heat to medium-low and simmer for 45 minutes until cooked and stew reach to desired thickness.
4. Serve straight away.

Nutrition Value:

- Calories: 156 Cal
- Fat: 3 g
- Carbs: 22 g
- Protein: 12 g
- Fiber: 5.1100 g

Mexican Lentil Soup

Preparation time: 5 minutes
Cooking time: 45 minutes
Servings: 6

Ingredients:

- 2 cups green lentils
- 1 medium red bell pepper, cored, diced
- 1 medium white onion, peeled, diced
- 2 cups diced tomatoes
- 8 ounces diced green chilies
- 2 celery stalks, diced
- 2 medium carrots, peeled, diced
- 1 ½ teaspoon minced garlic
- 1/2 teaspoon salt
- 1 tablespoon cumin
- 1/4 teaspoon smoked paprika
- 1 teaspoon oregano
- 1/8 teaspoon hot sauce
- 2 tablespoons olive oil
- 8 cups vegetable broth
- ¼ cup cilantro, for garnish
- 1 avocado, peeled, pitted, diced, for garnish

Method:

1. Take a large pot over medium heat, add oil and when hot, add all the vegetables, reserving tomatoes and chilies, and cook for 5 minutes until softened.
2. Then add garlic, stir in oregano, cumin, and paprika, and continue cooking for 1 minute.
3. Add lentils, tomatoes and green chilies, season with salt, pour in the broth and simmer the soup for 40 minutes until cooked.
4. When done, ladle soup into bowls, top with avocado and cilantro and serve straight away

Nutrition Value:

- Calories: 235 Cal
- Fat: 9 g
- Carbs: 32 g
- Protein: 9 g
- Fiber: 10 g

Curry Lentil Soup

Preparation time: 5 minutes
Cooking time: 40 minutes
Servings: 6

Ingredients:

- 1 cup brown lentils
- 1 medium white onion, peeled, chopped
- 28 ounces diced tomatoes
- 1 ½ teaspoon minced garlic
- 1 inch of ginger, grated
- 3 cups vegetable broth
- 1/2 teaspoon salt
- 2 tablespoons curry powder
- 1 teaspoon cumin
- 1/2 teaspoon cayenne
- 1 tablespoon olive oil
- 1 1/2 cups coconut milk, unsweetened
- ¼ cup chopped cilantro

Method:

1. Take a soup pot, place it over medium-high heat, add oil and when hot, add onion, stir in garlic and ginger and cook for 5 minutes until golden brown.
2. Then add all the ingredients except for milk and cilantro, stir until mixed and simmer for 25 minutes until lentils have cooked.
3. When done, stir in milk, cook for 5 minutes until thoroughly heated and then garnish the soup with cilantro.
4. Serve straight away

Nutrition Value:

- Calories: 269 Cal
- Fat: 15 g
- Carbs: 26 g
- Protein: 10 g
- Fiber: 10 g

Cream of Mushroom Soup

Preparation time: 5 minutes
Cooking time: 12 minutes
Servings: 6

Ingredients:

- 1 medium white onion, peeled, chopped
- 16 ounces button mushrooms, sliced
- 1 ½ teaspoon minced garlic
- 1/4 cup all-purpose flour
- 1/2 teaspoon ground black pepper
- 1 teaspoon dried thyme
- 1/4 teaspoon nutmeg
- 1/2 teaspoon salt
- 2 tablespoons vegan butter
- 4 cups vegetable broth
- 1 1/2 cups coconut milk, unsweetened

Method:

1. Take a large pot, place it over medium-high heat, add butter and when it melts, add onions and garlic, stir in garlic and cook for 5 minutes until softened and nicely brown.
2. Then sprinkle flour over vegetables, continue cooking for 1 minute, then add remaining ingredients, stir until mixed and simmer for 5 minutes until thickened.
3. Serve straight away

Nutrition Value:

- Calories: 120 Cal
- Fat: 7 g
- Carbs: 10 g
- Protein: 2 g
- Fiber: 6 g

Spinach and Cannellini Bean Stew

Preparation time: 10 minutes
Cooking time: 15 minutes
Servings: 6

Ingredients:

- 28 ounces cooked cannellini beans
- 24 ounces tomato passata
- 17 ounces spinach chopped
- ¼ teaspoon ground black pepper
- 2/3 teaspoon salt
- 1 ¼ teaspoon curry powder
- 1 cup cashew butter
- ¼ teaspoon cardamom
- 2 tablespoons olive oil
- 1 teaspoon salt
- ¼ cup cashews
- 2 tablespoons chopped basil
- 2 tablespoons chopped parsley

Method:

1. Take a large saucepan, place it over medium heat, add 1 tablespoon oil and when hot, add spinach and cook for 3 minutes until fried.
2. Then stir in butter and tomato passata until well mixed, bring the mixture to a near boil, add beans and season with ¼ teaspoon curry powder, black pepper, and salt.
3. Take a small saucepan, place it over medium heat, add remaining oil, stir in cashew, stir in salt and curry powder and cook for 4 minutes until roasted, set aside until required.
4. Transfer cooked stew into a bowl, top with roasted cashews, basil, and parsley, and then serve.

Nutrition Value:

- Calories: 242 Cal
- Fat: 10.2 g
- Carbs: 31 g
- Protein: 11 g
- Fiber: 8.5 g

Red Pepper and Tomato Soup

Preparation time: 10 minutes
Cooking time: 40 minutes
Servings: 4

Ingredients:

- 2 carrots, peeled, chopped
- 1 1/4 pounds red bell peppers, deseeded, sliced into quarters
- 1/2 of medium red onion, peeled, sliced into thin wedges
- 16 ounces small tomatoes, halved
- 1 tablespoon chopped basil
- 1/2 teaspoon salt
- 2 cups vegetable broth

Method:

1. Switch on the oven, then set it to 450 degrees F and let it preheat.
2. Then place all the vegetables in a single on a baking sheet lined with foil and roast for 40 minutes until the skins of peppers are slightly charred.
3. When done, remove the baking sheet from the oven, let them cool for 10 minutes, then peel the peppers and transfer all the vegetables into a blender.
4. Add basil and salt to the vegetables, pour in the broth, and puree the vegetables until smooth.
5. Serve straight away.

Nutrition Value:

- Calories: 77.4 Cal
- Fat: 1.8 g
- Carbs: 14.4 g
- Protein: 3.3 g
- Fiber: 3.3 g

Broccoli Cheese Soup

Preparation time: 10 minutes
Cooking time: 15 minutes
Servings: 4

Ingredients:

- 1 medium potato, peeled, diced
- 2 ribs celery, diced
- 1 medium white onion, peeled, diced
- 2 medium yellow summer squash, diced
- 1 medium carrot, peeled, diced
- 6 cups chopped broccoli florets
- 1 teaspoon minced garlic
- 1 bay leaf
- 1/3 teaspoon ground black pepper
- ¼ cup nutritional yeast
- 1 tablespoon lemon juice
- 2 tablespoons apple cider vinegar
- ½ cup cashews
- 3 cups of water

Method:

1. Take a large pot, place it over medium-high heat, add all the vegetables in it, except for florets, add bay leaf, pour in water and bring the mixture to boil.
2. Then switch heat to medium-low and simmer for 10 minutes until vegetables are tender.
3. Meanwhile, place broccoli florets in another pot, place it over medium-low heat and cook for 4 minutes or more until broccoli has steamed.
4. When done, remove broccoli from the pot, reserve 1 cup of its liquid, and set aside until required.
5. When vegetables have cooked, remove the bay leaf, add remaining ingredients in it, reserving broccoli and its liquid, and then puree the soup by using an immersion blender until smooth.
6. Then add steamed broccoli along with its liquid, stir well and serve straight away.

Nutrition Value:

- Calories: 223.5 Cal
- Fat: 12 g
- Carbs: 19 g
- Protein: 10.6 g
- Fiber: 1.7 g

Cauliflower and Horseradish Soup

Preparation time: 5 minutes
Cooking time: 20 minutes
Servings: 4

Ingredients:

- 2 medium potatoes, peeled, chopped
- 1 medium cauliflower, florets and stalk chopped
- 1 medium white onion, peeled, chopped
- 1 teaspoon minced garlic
- 2/3 teaspoon salt
- 1/3 teaspoon ground black pepper
- 4 teaspoons horseradish sauce
- 1 teaspoon dried thyme
- 3 cups vegetable broth
- 1 cup coconut milk, unsweetened

Method:

1. Place all the vegetables in a large pan, place it over medium-high heat, add thyme, pour in broth and milk and bring the mixture to boil.
2. Then switch heat to medium level, simmer the soup for 15 minutes and remove the pan from heat.
3. Puree the soup by using an immersion blender until smooth, season with salt and black pepper, and serve straight away.

Nutrition Value:

- Calories: 160 Cal
- Fat: 2.6 g
- Carbs: 31 g
- Protein: 6 g
- Fiber: 6 g

Black Bean and Quinoa Stew

Preparation time: 10 minutes
Cooking time: 6 hours
Servings: 6

Ingredients:

- 1 pound black beans, dried, soaked overnight
- 3/4 cup quinoa, uncooked
- 1 medium red bell pepper, cored, chopped
- 1 medium red onion, peeled, diced
- 1 medium green bell pepper, cored, chopped
- 28-ounce diced tomatoes
- 2 dried chipotle peppers
- 1 ½ teaspoon minced garlic
- 2/3 teaspoon sea salt
- 2 teaspoons red chili powder
- 1/3 teaspoon ground black pepper
- 1 teaspoon coriander powder
- 1 dried cinnamon stick
- 1/4 cup cilantro
- 7 cups of water

Method:

1. Switch on the slow cooker, add all the ingredients in it, except for salt, and stir until mixed.
2. Shut the cooker with lid and cook for 6 hours at a high heat setting until cooked.
3. When done, stir salt into the stew until mixed, remove cinnamon sticks and serve.

Nutrition Value:

- Calories: 308 Cal
- Fat: 2 g
- Carbs: 70 g
- Protein: 23 g
- Fiber: 32 g

Kimchi Stew

Preparation time: 10 minutes
Cooking time: 25 minutes
Servings: 4

Ingredients:

- 1 pound tofu, extra-firm, pressed, cut into 1-inch pieces
- 4 cups napa cabbage kimchi, vegan, chopped
- 1 small white onion, peeled, diced
- 2 cups sliced shiitake mushroom caps
- 1 ½ teaspoon minced garlic
- 2 tablespoons soy sauce
- 2 tablespoons olive oil, divided
- 4 cups vegetable broth
- 2 tablespoons chopped scallions

Method:

1. Take a large pot, place it over medium heat, add 1 tablespoon oil and when hot, add tofu pieces in a single layer and cook for 10 minutes until browned on all sides.
2. When cooked, transfer tofu pieces to a plate, add remaining oil to the pot and when hot, add onion and cook for 5 minutes until soft.
3. Stir in garlic, cook for 1 minute until fragrant, stir in kimchi, continue cooking for 2 minutes, then add mushrooms and pour in broth.
4. Switch heat to medium-high level, bring the mixture to boil, then switch heat to medium-low level and simmer for 10 minutes until mushrooms are softened.
5. Stir in tofu, taste to adjust seasoning, and garnish with scallions.
6. Serve straight away.

Nutrition Value:

- Calories: 153 Cal
- Fat: 8.2 g
- Carbs: 25 g
- Protein: 8.4 g
- Fiber: 2.6 g

Fennel and Chickpeas Provençal

Preparation time: 10 minutes
Cooking time: 50 minutes
Servings: 4

Ingredients:

- 15 ounces cooked chickpeas
- 3 fennel bulbs, sliced
- 1 medium onion, peeled, sliced
- 15 ounces diced tomatoes
- 10 black olives, pitted, cured
- 10 Kalamata olives, pitted
- 1 ½ teaspoon minced garlic
- 1 teaspoon salt
- 1/8 teaspoon ground black pepper
- 1 teaspoon Herbes de Provence
- 1/2 teaspoon red pepper flakes
- 2 tablespoons olive oil
- 1/2 cup water
- 2 tablespoons chopped parsley

Method:

1. Take a saucepan, place it over medium-high heat, add oil and when hot, add onion, fennel, and garlic and cook for 20 minutes until softened.
2. Then add remaining ingredients except for olives and chickpeas, bring the mixture to boil, switch heat to medium-low level and simmer for 15 minutes.
3. Then add remaining ingredients, cook for 10 minutes until hot, garnish stew with parsley and serve.

Nutrition Value:

- Calories: 395 Cal
- Fat: 13 g
- Carbs: 56 g
- Protein: 16 g
- Fiber: 13 g

Chapter 4: Salads

Cranberry and Quinoa Salad

Preparation time: 15 minutes
Cooking time: 0 minute
Servings: 6

Ingredients:

- 2 cups cooked quinoa
- 1/4 cup chopped red onion
- 1/2 cup shredded carrots
- 1/2 cup dried cranberries
- 1/2 cup diced green bell pepper
- 4 tablespoons chopped cilantro
- 1 ½ teaspoon curry powder
- 2/3 teaspoon salt
- 1/3 teaspoon ground black pepper
- 1/8 teaspoon cumin
- 1/3 cup toasted sliced almonds
- 4 tablespoons pepitas
- Olive oil as needed for drizzling
- 1 lime, juiced
- Lime, sliced into wedges

Method:

1. Place all the ingredients in a large bowl, toss until well combined and let the salad refrigerate for 15 minutes.
2. Serve straight away.

Nutrition Value:

- Calories: 199 Cal
- Fat: 6 g
- Carbs: 30 g
- Protein: 6 g
- Fiber: 4 g

Zucchini Salad

Preparation time: 10 minutes
Cooking time: 15 minutes
Servings: 4

Ingredients:

- 2 cups cubed zucchini
- 1 tablespoon chopped mint
- 1 small white onion, peeled, sliced
- ½ of a lemon, juiced
- 1 teaspoon minced garlic
- 2 tablespoons olive oil
- 1/8 teaspoon ground white pepper
- ¼ teaspoon salt
- 1/8 teaspoon ground turmeric
- 1/2 teaspoon ground cumin
- 7 saffron threads

Method:

1. Take a skillet pan, place it over medium heat, add oil and when hot, add onion and garlic, and cook for 4 minutes until softened.
2. Then add remaining ingredients, except for salt, black pepper, lime juice, and mint, stir until mixed and cook for 8 minutes until zucchini is tender-crisp.
3. When done, let the salad cool for 10 minutes, then season with salt and black pepper, drizzle with lemon juice, sprinkle with mint and serve.

Nutrition Value:

- Calories: 93 Cal
- Fat: 7.2 g
- Carbs: 7.8 g
- Protein: 1.6 g
- Fiber: 1.9 g

Grilled Corn Salad Bowl

Preparation time: 10 minutes
Cooking time: 0 minute
Servings: 4

Ingredients:

- ½ cup of beluga lentils, cooked
- 2 ears of fresh corn, grilled
- ½ cup pickled onions
- 1 medium avocado, peeled, sliced
- 1 green chili, chopped
- 2 cups arugula
- ¼ teaspoon ground black pepper
- 2/3 teaspoon salt
- 2 limes, juiced
- 4 tablespoons olive oil
- 10 basil leaves, chopped
- ¼ cup pine nuts, toasted

Method:

1. Place all the ingredients in the bowl, except for lime juice and oil, and stir until mixed.
2. Drizzle with lime juice and oil, toss until mixed and serve.

Nutrition Value:

- Calories: 179 Cal
- Fat: 6.3 g
- Carbs: 30 g
- Protein: 6.3 g
- Fiber: 5.5 g

Pear, Pomegranate and Roasted Butternut Squash Salad

Preparation time: 10 minutes
Cooking time: 10 minutes
Servings: 3

Ingredients:

- 1 medium butternut squash, peeled, cut into noodles
- 5 ounces of arugula
- 1 large pear, spiralized
- ¾ cup pomegranate seeds
- 2/3 teaspoon salt
- 1/3 teaspoon ground black pepper
- 3/4 cup chopped walnuts

For the Vinaigrette:

- ½ teaspoon minced garlic
- 1 teaspoon white sesame seeds
- ¼ teaspoon ground black pepper
- 1 tablespoon maple syrup
- 1 tablespoon olive oil
- 1 tablespoon soy sauce
- 1 tablespoon sesame oil
- 2 tablespoons apple cider vinegar

Method:

1. Place butternut squash noodles on a baking sheet, spray with oil, season with salt and black pepper and roast for 10 minutes at 400 degrees F until cooked.
2. Meanwhile, prepare the vinaigrette and for this, place all its ingredients in a bowl and whisk until combined.
3. When done, place pear, walnuts, and arugula in a large bowl, then add squash, drizzle with vinaigrette and toss until combined.
4. Serve straight away.

Nutrition Value:

- Calories: 423 Cal
- Fat: 29 g
- Carbs: 38 g
- Protein: 8 g
- Fiber: 6 g

Greens Salad with Black Eyed Peas

Preparation time: 5 minutes
Cooking time: 6 minutes
Servings: 3

Ingredients:

- 2 cups cooked black-eyed peas, cooked
- 1/2 cup cooked quinoa
- 3 cups chopped purple cabbage
- 5 cups chopped kale
- 1/2 of a shallot, peeled, chopped
- 1 1/2 cup shredded carrot
- 1 teaspoon minced garlic
- 1/2 teaspoon sea salt
- 1/3 teaspoon ground black pepper
- 1 tablespoon apple cider vinegar and more as needed
- 1 tablespoon lemon juice
- 2 tablespoons olive oil

Method:

1. Sauté garlic, shallot, and cabbage in 1 tablespoon for 2 minutes over medium heat, then add remaining oil along with kale, season with salt, and cook for 4 minutes until kale has wilted.
2. Transfer the vegetables to a bowl, add remaining ingredients and toss until combined.
3. Serve straight away

Nutrition Value:

- Calories: 166 Cal
- Fat: 5.3 g
- Carbs: 28.6 g
- Protein: 4.2 g
- Fiber: 6.7 g

Chopped Kale Power Salad

Preparation time: 10 minutes
Cooking time: 40 minutes
Servings: 4

Ingredients:

For the Salad:
- 15 ounces cooked chickpeas
- 8 cups chopped kale
- 6 cups diced sweet potatoes
- 1 large avocado, pitted, diced
- 1/4 cup chopped red onion
- 2 teaspoons and 1 tablespoon olive oil, divided
- 1/4 teaspoon ground black pepper
- 3/4 teaspoons salt, divided
- 1/3 cup chopped almonds
- 1/2 of a large lemon, juiced
- 1/3 cup dried cranberries

For the Lemon Tahini Dressing:
- 1/2 cup tahini
- 1/4 teaspoon salt
- 1 lemon juiced
- 6 tablespoons warm water

Method:

1. Place diced sweet potatoes on a sheet pan, drizzle with 2 teaspoon oil, season with ¼ teaspoon black pepper and ½ teaspoon salt and bake for 40 minutes at 375 degrees F until roasted, tossing halfway.
2. Meanwhile, place chopped kale in a bowl, drizzle with lemon juice and remaining oil, season with remaining salt, toss until combined, and massage the leaves for 1 minute.
3. Prepare the dressing and for this, place all of its ingredients in a bowl and whisk until combined.
4. Top kale salad with sweet potatoes, drizzle with tahini dressing, and serve.

Nutrition Value:
- Calories: 82 Cal
- Fat: 2 g
- Carbs: 15 g
- Protein: 2 g
- Fiber: 1 g

Kale Slaw

Preparation time: 10 minutes
Cooking time: 0 minute
Servings: 4

Ingredients:

For the Salad:
- ½ small head of cabbage, shredded
- ¼ cup mixed herbs
- ¼ of a medium red onion, peeled, sliced
- 1 small bunch of kale, cut into ribbons

For the Dressing:
- 1 teaspoon minced garlic
- ¼ teaspoon ground black pepper
- ¼ teaspoon salt
- ¼ teaspoon red chili flakes
- ¼ cup olive oil
- 1 lemon, juiced

For the Topping:
- 1 teaspoon hemp seeds
- 1 teaspoon sunflower
- 1 teaspoon pumpkin seeds

Method:

1. Prepare the dressing and for this, place all of its ingredients in a small bowl and whisk until smooth.
2. Take a large bowl, place all the ingredients for the salad in it, top with prepared dressing and toss until well coated.
3. Garnish the salad with all the seeds and then serve.

Nutrition Value:
- Calories: 76 Cal
- Fat: 7.1 g
- Carbs: 4 g
- Protein: 0.7 g
- Fiber: 1 g

Butternut Squash Quinoa Salad

Preparation time: 10 minutes
Cooking time: 25 minutes
Servings: 4

Ingredients:

For the Salad:

- 1 cup quinoa, cooked
- 3 cups butternut squash, chopped
- 1/3 cup dried cranberries
- 1/3 cup chopped red onion
- 2/3 teaspoon salt
- 1/3 teaspoon ground black pepper
- 3 tablespoons toasted pumpkin seeds
- 1 tablespoon olive oil

For the Dressing:

- ½ teaspoon minced garlic
- 1/3 teaspoon salt
- 1/3 teaspoon ground black pepper
- 1 teaspoon honey
- 1/4 cup balsamic vinegar
- 1 teaspoon Dijon mustard
- 1/2 cup olive oil

Method:

1. Spread butternut squash on a baking sheet, drizzle with oil, season with black pepper and salt and bake for 25 minutes until roasted and tender.
2. Meanwhile, prepare the dressing and for this, place all of its ingredients in a bowl and whisk until smooth.
3. When done, let squash for 10 minutes, then place them in a bowl, add remaining ingredients for the salad in it, drizzle with dressing and toss until coated.
4. Refrigerate the salad for a minimum of 2 hours and then serve.

Nutrition Value:

- Calories: 385 Cal
- Fat: 25 g
- Carbs: 38 g
- Protein: 6.2 g
- Fiber: 8 g

Butternut Squash and Kale Salad

Preparation time: 10 minutes
Cooking time: 8 minutes
Servings: 4

Ingredients:

For the Salad:
- 6 cups butternut squash, spiralized
- 5 cups kale, chopped, steamed
- 1/3 cup pumpkin seeds
- 1/2 cup pomegranate seeds

For the Dressing:
- ½ teaspoon salt
- ½ teaspoon ground black pepper
- 1/2 teaspoon cinnamon
- 1 tablespoon maple syrup
- 1/2 teaspoon mustard
- 2 tablespoons apple cider vinegar
- 3 tablespoons olive oil

Method:
1. Place spiralized squash on a baking sheet, toss with olive oil and bake for 8 minutes at 400 degrees F until roasted.
2. When done, let squash cool for 10 minutes, then add it into a large bowl along with remaining ingredients for the salad and toss until mixed.
3. Prepare the dressing and for this, place all of its ingredients in a bowl and stir until combined.
4. Drizzle the dressing over the salad, toss until mixed, and then serve.

Nutrition Value:
- Calories: 200 Cal
- Fat: 5 g
- Carbs: 48 g
- Protein: 6 g
- Fiber: 4 g

Vegan Caesar Salad

Preparation time: 10 minutes
Cooking time: 30 minutes
Servings: 4

Ingredients:

- ½ cup chickpea croutons
- 10 ounces tofu, firmed, drain, dice
- 1 romaine lettuce, chopped
- 1 cup vegan Caesar dressing
- ¼ cup grated vegan Parmesan cheese

For the Dressing:

- ½ teaspoon garlic powder
- ½ teaspoon ground black pepper
- ½ teaspoon sweet paprika
- ½ teaspoon onion powder
- ½ teaspoon cumin
- ½ teaspoon dried thyme
- 3 tablespoons soy sauce
- 3 tablespoons water

Method:

1. Place tofu pieces on a baking sheet lined with baking paper and then bake for 30 minutes at 390 degrees F until golden brown on all sides, turning halfway.
2. Meanwhile, prepare the dressing and for this, place all of its ingredients in a bowl and whisk until smooth.
3. When tofu has roasted, let it cool for 5 minutes, then add to the bowl along with remaining ingredients for the salad, drizzle with prepared dressing and toss until combined.
4. Serve straight away.

Nutrition Value:

- Calories: 469 Cal
- Fat: 28 g
- Carbs: 86.5 g
- Protein: 38.5 g
- Fiber: 29 g

Tropical Radicchio Slaw

Preparation time: 15 minutes
Cooking time: 8 minutes
Servings: 6

Ingredients:
- 2 medium heads of radicchio, quartered
- 1/4 cup chopped basil leaves
- 2 cups chopped pineapple
- 1/2 teaspoon ground black pepper
- 1/2 teaspoon salt
- 2 tablespoons olive oil
- 2 tablespoons orange juice

Method:
1. Brush radicchio with oil on both sides and then grill for 8 minutes until tender, turning halfway.
2. When grilled, let radicchio cool for 10 minutes, then slice them thinly and place them in a bowl.
3. Add remaining ingredients, toss until combined, and serve.

Nutrition Value:
- Calories: 40 Cal
- Fat: 2 g
- Carbs: 5 g
- Protein: 0 g
- Fiber: 1 g

Heirloom Tomato Salad

Preparation time: 10 minutes
Cooking time: 0 minute
Servings: 6

Ingredients:

For the Salad:
- 1 pound heirloom tomatoes, cut into wedges
- ½ teaspoon salt
- ½ teaspoon ground black pepper
- ¼ cup basil leaves, for serving

For the Dressing:
- 2 cups grape tomatoes, halved
- ¼ teaspoon ground black pepper
- ½ teaspoon salt
- 2 tablespoons chopped chives
- 1 teaspoon honey
- 1/4 cup olive oil
- 2 tablespoons apple cider vinegar

Method:
1. Prepare the dressing for this, whisk together honey, vinegar, oil, salt, and black pepper until combined, then add chives and tomatoes and toss until combined.
2. Prepare the salad and for this, place tomatoes on a plate, season with salt and black pepper, drizzle with the dressing and top with basil.
3. Serve straight away.

Nutrition Value:
- Calories: 105 Cal
- Fat: 9.5 g
- Carbs: 6 g
- Protein: 1 g
- Fiber: 1 g

Spiralized Zucchini and Carrot Salad

Preparation time: 10 minutes
Cooking time: 0 minute
Servings: 6

Ingredients:

For the Salad:
- 2 scallions, sliced
- 2 large zucchini. spiralized
- 1 red chile, sliced
- 1 large carrot, spiralized

For the Dressing:
- 1 1/2 teaspoon grated ginger
- 2 teaspoons brown sugar
- 1/4 cup lime juice
- 1 tablespoon soy sauce
- 2 tablespoons toasted peanut oil

For Toppings:
- 1/2 cup chopped peanuts, roasted
- 1/3 cup chopped cilantro

Method:

1. Prepare the dressing and for this, place all of its ingredients in a bowl and whisk until combined.
2. Take a large bowl, place all the ingredients for the salad in it, stir until mixed, then drizzle with the dressing and toss until coated.
3. Top the salad with nuts and cilantro and then serve straight away.

Nutrition Value:
- Calories: 150 Cal
- Fat: 11 g
- Carbs: 11 g
- Protein: 5 g
- Fiber: 3 g

Lemon, Basil and Orzo Salad

Preparation time: 10 minutes
Cooking time: 0 minute
Servings: 4

Ingredients:

For the Salad:
- 1 cup orzo pasta, cooked
- 2 cups sliced cucumbers
- 1 cup cherry tomatoes, halved
- 1 cup baby arugula

For the Dressing:
- 2 cloves of garlic, peeled
- 1 lemon, zested
- 1 cup basil
- 1/3 cup olive oil
- ¼ teaspoon ground black pepper
- ½ teaspoon salt
- 2 tablespoons lemon juice

Method:
1. Prepare the dressing, and for this, place all of its ingredients in a food processor and pulse until smooth.
2. Take a large bowl, place orzo pasta in it, add prepared dressing in it, toss until mixed, then add remaining ingredients for the salad in it and toss until just mixed.
3. Serve straight away.

Nutrition Value:
- Calories: 233 Cal
- Fat: 15 g
- Carbs: 24 g
- Protein: 4.5 g
- Fiber: 3 g

Kohlrabi Slaw

Preparation time: 10 minutes
Cooking time: 0 minute
Servings: 4

Ingredients:

For the Citrus Dressing:
- 1/2 teaspoon salt
- 1/4 cup honey
- 1 tablespoon rice wine vinegar
- ¼ cup of orange juice
- 2 tablespoons lime juice
- 1/4 cup olive oil

For the Salad:
- 6 cups kohlrabi, trimmed, peeled, cut into matchsticks
- ½ of a jalapeno, minced
- 1 orange, juiced, zested
- ½ cup chopped cilantro
- 1 lime, juiced, zested
- 1/4 cup chopped scallion

Method:
1. Prepare the dressing and for this, place all of its ingredients in a small bowl and whisk until smooth.
2. Take a large bowl, place all the ingredients for the salad in it, top with prepared dressing and toss until well coated.
3. Top the salad with almonds and then serve straight away.

Nutrition Value:
- Calories: 109.4 Cal
- Fat: 4.8 g
- Carbs: 10.8 g
- Protein: 4.4 g
- Fiber: 4.4 g

Chapter 5: Beans and Grains

Stuffed Peppers

Preparation time: 10 minutes
Cooking time: 20 minutes
Servings: 4

Ingredients:

- 2 green onions, sliced
- 2 green bell peppers, halved, cored
- 1 large tomato, diced
- 1/2 cup Arborio rice, cooked
- ¼ teaspoon ground black pepper
- 1 teaspoon Italian seasoning
- 1 teaspoon salt
- 1 teaspoon dried basil
- 1 tablespoon olive oil
- 1 cup of water
- 1/2 cup crumbled vegan feta cheese

Method:

1. Prepare the peppers and for this, cut them in half, then remove the seeds and roast them on a greased baking sheet for 20 minutes at 400 degrees F until tender.
2. Meanwhile, heat oil in a skillet pan over medium-high heat and when hot, add onion, season with seasonings and herbs, and cook for 3 minutes.
3. Add tomatoes, stir well, cook for 5 minutes, then stir in rice and cook for 3 minutes until heated.
4. When done, remove the pan from heat, stir in cheese, and stuff the mixture into roasted peppers.
5. Serve straight away.

Nutrition Value:

- Calories: 385 Cal
- Fat: 15.2 g
- Carbs: 52.6 g
- Protein: 10.8 g
- Fiber: 4.5 g

Quinoa and Black Bean Chili

Preparation time: 10 minutes
Cooking time: 32 minutes
Servings: 10

Ingredients:

- 1 cup quinoa, cooked
- 38 ounces cooked black beans
- 1 medium white onion, peeled, chopped
- 1 cup of frozen corn
- 1 green bell pepper, deseeded, chopped
- 1 zucchini, chopped
- 1 tablespoon minced chipotle peppers in adobo sauce
- 1 red bell pepper, deseeded, chopped
- 1 jalapeno pepper, deseeded, minced
- 28 ounces crushed tomatoes
- 2 teaspoons minced garlic
- 1/3 teaspoon ground black pepper
- ¾ teaspoon salt
- 1 teaspoon dried oregano
- 1 tablespoon red chili powder
- 1 tablespoon ground cumin
- 1 tablespoon olive oil
- 1/4 cup chopped cilantro

Method:

1. Take a large pot, place it over medium heat, add oil and when hot, add onion and cook for 5 minutes.
2. Then stir in garlic, cumin, and chili powder, cook for 1 minute, add remaining ingredients except for corn and quinoa, stir well and simmer for 20 minutes at medium-low heat until cooked.
3. Then stir in corn and quinoa, cook for 5 minutes until hot and then top with cilantro.
4. Serve straight away.

Nutrition Value:

- Calories: 233 Cal
- Fat: 3.5 g
- Carbs: 42 g
- Protein: 11.5 g
- Fiber: 11.8 g

Sweet Potato and White Bean Skillet

Preparation time: 10 minutes
Cooking time: 45 minutes
Servings: 4

Ingredients:

- 1 large bunch of kale, chopped
- 2 large sweet potatoes, peeled, ¼-inch cubes
- 12 ounces cannellini beans
- 1 small onion, peeled, diced
- 1/8 teaspoon red pepper flakes
- 1 teaspoon salt
- 1 teaspoon cumin
- ½ teaspoon ground black pepper
- 1 teaspoon curry powder
- 1 1/2 tablespoons coconut oil
- 6 ounces coconut milk, unsweetened

Method:

1. Take a large skillet pan, place it over medium heat, add ½ tablespoon oil and when it melts, add onion and cook for 5 minutes.
2. Then stir in sweet potatoes, stir well, cook for 5 minutes, then season with all the spices, cook for 1 minute and remove the pan from heat.
3. Take another pan, add remaining oil in it, place it over medium heat and when oil melts, add kale, season with some salt and black pepper, stir well, pour in the milk and cook for 15 minutes until tender.
4. Then add beans, beans, and red pepper, stir until mixed and cook for 5 minutes until hot.
5. Serve straight away.

Nutrition Value:

- Calories: 263 Cal
- Fat: 4 g
- Carbs: 44 g
- Protein: 13 g
- Fiber: 12 g

Zucchini Risotto

Preparation time: 10 minutes
Cooking time: 30 minutes
Servings: 6

Ingredients:

- 2 cups Arborio rice
- 10 sun-dried tomatoes, chopped
- 1 medium white onion, peeled, chopped
- 1 tablespoon chopped basil leaves
- 1/2 medium zucchini, sliced
- 1 teaspoon dried thyme
- 1/3 teaspoon ground black pepper
- 1 tablespoon vegan butter
- 6 tablespoons grated vegan Parmesan cheese
- 7 cups vegetable broth, hot

Method:

1. Take a large pot, place it over medium heat, add butter and when it melts, add onion and cook for 2 minutes.
2. Stir in rice, cook for another 2 minutes until toasted, and then stir in broth, 1 cup at a time until absorbed completely and creamy mixture comes together.
3. Then stir in remaining ingredients until combined, taste to adjust seasoning and serve.

Nutrition Value:

- Calories: 363 Cal
- Fat: 4.1 g
- Carbs: 71.2 g
- Protein: 9.1 g
- Fiber: 3.1 g

Black Beans and Rice

Preparation time: 10 minutes
Cooking time: 30 minutes
Servings: 4

Ingredients:

- 3/4 cup white rice
- 1 medium white onion, peeled, chopped
- 3 1/2 cups cooked black beans
- 1 teaspoon minced garlic
- 1/4 teaspoon cayenne pepper
- 1 teaspoon ground cumin
- 1 teaspoon olive oil
- 1 1/2 cups vegetable broth

Method:

1. Take a large pot over medium-high heat, add oil and when hot, add onion and garlic and cook for 4 minutes until sauté.
2. Then stir in rice, cook for 2 minutes, pour in the broth, bring it to a boil, switch heat to the low level and cook for 20 minutes until tender.
3. Stir in remaining ingredients, cook for 2 minutes, and then serve straight away.

Nutrition Value:

- Calories: 140 Cal
- Fat: 0.9 g
- Carbs: 27.1 g
- Protein: 6.3 g
- Fiber: 6.2 g

Falafel

Preparation time: 10 minutes
Cooking time: 30 minutes
Servings: 4

Ingredients:
- ¼ cup and 1 tablespoon olive oil
- 1 cup chickpeas, cooked
- ½ cup chopped parsley
- ½ cup chopped red onion
- ½ cup chopped cilantro
- 2 teaspoons minced garlic
- ½ teaspoon ground black pepper
- ¼ teaspoon ground cinnamon
- 1 teaspoon of sea salt
- ½ teaspoon ground cumin

Method:
1. Place all the ingredients in a food processor, reserving ¼ cup oil, and pulse until smooth.
2. Shape the mixture into small patties, place them on a rimmed baking sheet, greased with remaining oil and bake for 30 minutes until cooked and roasted on both sides, turning halfway through.
3. Serve straight away.

Nutrition Value:
- Calories: 354 Cal
- Fat: 20.7 g
- Carbs: 34.6 g
- Protein: 11 g
- Fiber: 7 g

Zoodles with White Beans

Preparation time: 10 minutes
Cooking time: 20 minutes
Servings: 4

Ingredients:

- 15 ounces cooked cannellini beans
- 2 medium zucchinis, spiralized into noodles
- 3 teaspoons minced garlic
- 1 cup chopped Roma tomatoes
- 2/3 teaspoon salt
- 1/8 teaspoon red pepper flakes
- 1/4 cup olive oil
- 1/4 cup chopped parsley
- 4 ounces whole-grain spaghetti, cooked

Method:

1. Cook the pasta, drain it, transfer it into a bowl, add zucchini noodles and toss until mixed.
2. Take a pot, place it over low heat, add oil, garlic, and red pepper flakes, stir until cook for 5 minutes until garlic is golden brown.
3. Then add all the ingredients, except for parsley and salt, toss until mixed and cook for 5 minutes until thoroughly heated.
4. When done, season with salt, top with parsley and serve.

Nutrition Value:

- Calories: 301 Cal
- Fat: 15 g
- Carbs: 34 g
- Protein: 11 g
- Fiber: 7 g

Lentil and Chickpea Salad

Preparation time: 10 minutes
Cooking time: 0 minute
Servings: 4

Ingredients:

For the Lemon Dressing:
- ¼ cup lemon juice
- 2 tablespoons olive oil
- 1 teaspoon Dijon mustard
- 1 teaspoon honey or maple syrup
- ½ teaspoon minced garlic
- ¼ teaspoon of sea salt
- ¼ teaspoon ground black pepper

For the Salad:
- 2 cups French green lentils, cooked
- 1 ½ cups cooked chickpeas
- 1 medium avocado, pitted, sliced
- 1 big bunch of radishes, chopped
- ¼ cup chopped mint and dill
- Crumbled vegan feta cheese as needed

Method:
1. Prepare the dressing and for this, place all of its ingredients in a bowl and whisk until combined.
2. Take a large bowl, place all the ingredients for the salad in it, drizzle with the dressing and toss until combined.
3. Serve straight away.

Nutrition Value:
- Calories: 377 Cal
- Fat: 11.1 g
- Carbs: 53.4 g
- Protein: 19.2 g
- Fiber: 10.1 g

Rice Stuffed Jalapeños

Preparation time: 5 minutes
Cooking time: 15 minutes
Servings: 6

Ingredients:

- 3 medium-sized potatoes, peeled, cubed, boiled
- 2 large carrots, peeled, chopped, boiled
- 3 tablespoons water
- 1/4 teaspoon onion powder
- 1 teaspoons salt
- 1/2 cup nutritional yeast
- 1/4 teaspoon garlic powder
- 1 lime, juiced
- 3 tablespoons water
- Cooked rice as needed
- 3 jalapeños pepper, halved
- 1 red bell pepper, sliced, for garnish
- ½ cup vegetable broth

Method:

1. Place boiled vegetables in a food processor, pour in broth and pulse until smooth.
2. Add garlic powder, onion powder, salt, water, and lime juice, pulse until combined, then add yeast and blend until smooth.
3. Tip the mixture in a bowl, add rice, and stir until incorporated.
4. Cut each jalapeno into half lengthwise, brush them with oil, season them with some salt, stuff them with rice mixture and bake them for 20 minutes at 400 degrees F until done.
5. Serve straight away.

Nutrition Value:

- Calories: 148 Cal
- Fat: 3.7 g
- Carbs: 12.2 g
- Protein: 2 g
- Fiber: 2 g

Quinoa Meatballs

Preparation time: 10 minutes
Cooking time: 35 minutes
Servings: 4

Ingredients:

- 1 cup quinoa, cooked
- 1 tablespoon flax meal
- 1 cup diced white onion
- 1 ½ teaspoon minced garlic
- 1/2 teaspoon salt
- 1 teaspoon dried oregano
- 1 teaspoon lemon zest
- 1 teaspoon paprika
- 1 teaspoon dried basil
- 3 tablespoons water
- 2 tablespoons olive oil
- 1 cup grated vegan mozzarella cheese
- Marinara sauce as needed for serving

Method:

1. Place flax meal in a bowl, stir in water and set aside until required.
2. Take a large skillet pan, place it over medium heat, add 1 tablespoon oil and when hot, add onion and cook for 2 minutes.
3. Stir in all the spices and herbs, then stir in quinoa until combined and cook for 2 minutes.
4. Transfer quinoa mixture in a bowl, add flax meal mixture, lemon zest, and cheese, stir until well mixed and then shape the mixture into twelve 1 ½ inch balls.
5. Arrange balls on a baking sheet lined with parchment paper, refrigerate the balls for 30 minutes and then bake for 20 minutes at 400 degrees F.
6. Serve balls with marinara sauce.

Nutrition Value:

- Calories: 100 Cal
- Fat: 100 g
- Carbs: 100 g
- Protein: 100 g
- Fiber: 100 g

Tomato, Kale, and White Bean Skillet

Preparation time: 10 minutes
Cooking time: 10 minutes
Servings: 4

Ingredients:

- 30 ounces cooked cannellini beans
- 3.5 ounces sun-dried tomatoes, packed in oil, chopped
- 6 ounces kale, chopped
- 1 teaspoon minced garlic
- 1/4 teaspoon ground black pepper
- 1/4 teaspoon salt
- 1/2 tablespoon dried basil
- 1/8 teaspoon red pepper flakes
- 1 tablespoon apple cider vinegar
- 1 tablespoon olive oil
- 2 tablespoons oil from sun-dried tomatoes

Method:

1. Prepare the dressing and for this, place basil, black pepper, salt, vinegar, and red pepper flakes in a small bowl, add oil from sun-dried tomatoes and whisk until combined.
2. Take a skillet pan, place it over medium heat, add olive oil and when hot, add garlic and cook for 1 minute until fragrant.
3. Add kale, splash with some water and cook for 3 minutes until kale leaves have wilted.
4. Add tomatoes and beans, stir well and cook for 3 minutes until heated.
5. Remove pan from heat, drizzle with the prepared dressing, toss until mixed and serve.

Nutrition Value:

- Calories: 264 Cal
- Fat: 12 g
- Carbs: 38 g
- Protein: 9 g
- Fiber: 13 g

Chickpea Fajitas

Preparation time: 10 minutes
Cooking time: 30 minutes
Servings: 4

Ingredients:

For the Chickpea Fajitas:
- 1 1/2 cups cooked chickpeas
- 1 medium white onion, peeled, sliced
- 2 medium green bell peppers, cored, sliced
- 1 tablespoon fajita seasoning
- 2 tablespoons olive oil

For the Cream:
- 1/2 cup cashews, soaked
- 1 clove of garlic, peeled
- ½ teaspoon salt
- 1/2 teaspoon ground cumin
- 1/4 cup lime juice
- 1/4 cup water
- 1 tablespoon olive oil

To serve:
- Sliced avocado for topping
- Chopped lettuce for topping
- 4 flour tortillas
- Chopped tomatoes for topping
- Salsa for topping
- Chopped cilantro for topping

Method:
1. Prepare chickpeas and for this, whisk together seasoning and oil until combined, add onion, pepper, and chickpeas, toss until well coated, then spread them in a baking sheet and roast for 30 minutes at 400 degrees F until crispy and browned, stirring halfway.
2. Meanwhile, prepare the cream and for this, place all of its ingredients in a food processor and pulse until smooth, set aside until required.
3. When chickpeas and vegetables have roasted, top them evenly on tortillas, then top them evenly with avocado, lettuce, tomatoes, salsa, and cilantro and serve.

Nutrition Value:
- Calories: 391 Cal
- Fat: 16 g
- Carbs: 43 g
- Protein: 8 g
- Fiber: 9 g

Mexican Stuffed Peppers

Preparation time: 10 minutes
Cooking time: 40 minutes
Servings: 4

Ingredients:

- 2 cups cooked rice
- 1/2 cup chopped onion
- 15 ounces cooked black beans
- 4 large green bell peppers, destemmed, cored
- 1 tablespoon olive oil
- 1 tablespoon salt
- 14.5-ounce diced tomatoes
- 1/2 teaspoon ground cumin
- 1 teaspoon garlic salt
- 1 teaspoon red chili powder
- 1/2 teaspoon salt
- 2 cups shredded vegan Mexican cheese blend

Method:

1. Boil the bell peppers in salty water for 5 minutes until softened and then set aside until required.
2. Heat oil over medium heat in a skillet pan, then add onion and cook for 10 minutes until softened.
3. Transfer the onion mixture in a bowl, add remaining ingredients, reserving ½ cup cheese blended, stir until mixed, and then fill this mixture into the boiled peppers.
4. Arrange the peppers in the square baking dish, sprinkle them with remaining cheese and bake for 30 minutes at 350 degrees F.
5. Serve straight away.

Nutrition Value:

- Calories: 509 Cal
- Fat: 22.8 g
- Carbs: 55.5 g
- Protein: 24 g
- Fiber: 12 g

Lentil, Rice and Vegetable Bake

Preparation time: 10 minutes
Cooking time: 40 minutes
Servings: 6

Ingredients:

- 1/2 cup white rice, cooked
- 1 cup red lentils, cooked
- 1/3 cup chopped carrots
- 1 medium tomato, chopped
- 1 small onion, peeled, chopped
- 1/3 cup chopped zucchini
- 1/3 cup chopped celery
- 1 ½ teaspoon minced garlic
- ½ teaspoon ground black pepper
- 1 teaspoon dried basil
- 1 teaspoon ground cumin
- 1 teaspoon dried oregano
- ½ teaspoon salt
- 1 teaspoon olive oil
- 8 ounces tomato sauce

Method:

1. Take a skillet pan, place it over medium heat, add oil and when hot, add onion and garlic, and cook for 5 minutes.
2. Then add remaining vegetables, season with salt, black pepper, and half of each cumin, oregano and basil and cook for 5 minutes until vegetables are tender.
3. Take a casserole dish, place lentils and rice in it, top with vegetables, spread with tomato sauce and sprinkle with remaining cumin, oregano, and basil, and bake for 30 minutes until bubbly.
4. Serve straight away.

Nutrition Value:

- Calories: 187 Cal
- Fat: 1.5 g
- Carbs: 35.1 g
- Protein: 9.7 g
- Fiber: 8.1 g

Mediterranean Chickpea Casserole

Preparation time: 10 minutes
Cooking time: 60 minutes
Servings: 4

Ingredients:

- 3 cups baby spinach
- 2 medium red onions, peeled, diced
- 2 1/2 cups tomatoes
- 3 cups cooked chickpeas
- 1 ½ teaspoon minced garlic
- 1/3 teaspoon ground black pepper
- 1 ¼ teaspoon salt
- 1/4 teaspoon allspice
- 1 tablespoon coconut sugar
- 1 teaspoon dried oregano
- 1/4 teaspoon cayenne
- 1/4 teaspoon cloves
- 2 bay leaves
- 1 tablespoon coconut oil
- 2 tablespoons olive oil
- 1 cup vegetable stock
- 1 lemon, juiced
- 2 ounces vegan feta cheese

Method:

1. Take a large skillet pan, place it over medium-high heat, add coconut oil and when it melts, add onion and cook for 5 minutes until softened.
2. Switch heat to medium-low level, stir in garlic, cook for 2 minutes, then stir in tomatoes, add all the spices and bay leaves, pour in the stock, stir until mixed and cook for 20 minutes.
3. Then stir in chickpeas, simmer cooking for 15 minutes until the cooking liquid has reduced by one-third, stir in spinach and cook for 3 minutes until it begins to wilt.
4. Then stir in olive oil, sugar and lemon juice, taste to adjust seasoning, and remove and discard bay leaves.
5. When done, top chickpeas with cheese, broil for 5 minutes until cheese has melted and golden brown, then garnish with parsley and serve.

Nutrition Value:

- Calories: 257.8 Cal
- Fat: 3.8 g
- Carbs: 47.1 g
- Protein: 10.3 g
- Fiber: 9.4 g

Black Bean Stuffed Sweet Potatoes

Preparation time: 15 minutes
Cooking time: 65 minutes
Servings: 4

Ingredients:

- 4 large sweet potatoes
- 15 ounces cooked black beans
- 1/2 teaspoon ground black pepper
- 1/2 of a medium red onion, peeled, diced
- 1/2 teaspoon sea salt
- 1/4 teaspoon onion powder
- 1/4 teaspoon garlic powder
- 1/4 teaspoon red chili powder
- 1/4 teaspoon cumin
- 1 teaspoon lime juice
- 1 1/2 tablespoons olive oil
- 1/2 cup cashew cream sauce

Method:

1. Spread sweet potatoes on a baking tray greased with oil and bake for 65 minutes at 350 degrees F until tender.
2. Meanwhile, prepare the sauce, and for this, whisk together the cream sauce, black pepper and lime juice until combined, set aside until required.
3. When 10 minutes of the baking time of potatoes are left, heat a skillet pan with oil, then add onion and cook for 5 minutes until golden.
4. Then stir in spice, cook for another 3 minutes, stir in bean until combined and cook for 5 minutes until hot.
5. Let roasted sweet potatoes cool for 10 minutes, then cut them open, mash the flesh and top with bean mixture, cilantro and avocado, and then drizzle with cream sauce.
6. Serve straight away.

Nutrition Value:

- Calories: 387 Cal
- Fat: 16.1 g
- Carbs: 53 g
- Protein: 10.4 g
- Fiber: 17.6 g

Chapter 6: Vegetables

Pesto with Squash Ribbons and Fettuccine

Preparation time: 10 minutes
Cooking time: 0 minute
Servings: 4

Ingredients:

For the Pesto

- 1/3 cup pumpkin seeds, toasted
- 1 cup cilantro leaves
- 2 teaspoons chopped jalapeño, deseeded
- 1 teaspoon minced garlic
- 1 lime, juiced
- ½ teaspoon of sea salt
- ⅓ cup olive oil

For Pasta and Squash Ribbons

- 8 ounces fettuccine, whole-grain, cooked
- 2 small zucchinis
- 1 yellow squash

Method:

1. Prepare ribbons, and for this, slice zucchini and squash by using a vegetable peeler and then set aside until required.
2. Prepare pesto, and for this, place all its ingredients in a food processor and pulse for 2 minutes until blended.
3. Place vegetable ribbons in a bowl, add cooked pasta, then add prepared pesto and toss until well coated.
4. Serve straight away.

Nutrition Value:

- Calories: 351 Cal
- Fat: 20 g
- Carbs: 38.8 g
- Protein: 8 g
- Fiber: 6.1 g

Grilled Asparagus and Shiitake Tacos

Preparation time: 5 minutes
Cooking time: 15 minutes
Servings: 4

Ingredients:

- 8 ounces shiitake mushrooms, destemmed
- 1 bunch of green onions
- 2 teaspoons minced garlic
- 1 teaspoon ground chipotle chili
- 1/2 teaspoon salt
- 3 tablespoons olive oil
- 8 corn tortillas, warmed
- 4 lime wedges
- 1 cup guacamole
- ¼ cup cilantro sprigs
- 4 tablespoons hot sauce

Method:

1. Take a large baking dish, add garlic, salt, and chipotle and stir in oil until combined.
2. Add all the vegetables, toss until well coated, and then grill over medium heat until lightly charred, 6 minutes grilling time for asparagus, 5 minutes for onions and mushrooms.
3. When done, cut vegetables for 2-inch pieces, distribute them evenly between tortillas, top with cilantro, guacamole, and hot sauce and serve with lime wedges.

Nutrition Value:

- Calories: 350 Cal
- Fat: 21 g
- Carbs: 36 g
- Protein: 7 g
- Fiber: 11 g

Thai Tofu

Preparation time: 5 minutes
Cooking time: 7 minutes
Servings: 4

Ingredients:

- 14 ounces tofu, firm, drained, 3/4 inch cubed
- 1/3 cup chopped green onion
- 2 teaspoons grated ginger
- 3 tablespoons coconut flakes
- 1 teaspoon soy sauce
- 1 ½ teaspoon olive oil
- ¼ cup peanut butter
- ½ teaspoon sesame oil
- 1 teaspoon sesame seeds

Method:

1. Take a skillet pan, place it over medium-high heat. Reduce heat to medium, add both oils and when hot, add green onions and cook for 1 minute.
2. Then add tofu cubes, cook for 4 minutes and stir in soy sauce halfway.
3. Stir in ginger and peanut butter, stir gently until well incorporated, and then remove the pan from heat.
4. Sprinkle with sesame seeds and serve.

Nutrition Value:

- Calories: 285 Cal
- Fat: 20.5 g
- Carbs: 10.6 g
- Protein: 20.1 g
- Fiber: 4.3 g

Middle Eastern Salad Tacos

Preparation time: 10 minutes
Cooking time: 5 minutes
Servings: 3

Ingredients:

For the Spiced Chickpeas:
- 12 ounces cooked chickpeas
- ½ cup hummus
- ½ teaspoon salt
- 1 teaspoon cumin
- 1 teaspoon sumac
- 2 teaspoons olive oil
- 1 teaspoon sesame seeds
- 6 tortillas, warmed, about 6-inches
- Scallions for topping

For the Salad:
- 2 cucumbers, diced
- 1 tomato, diced
- ½ cup arugula
- ¼ teaspoon salt
- 1 teaspoon ground coriander
- 2 tablespoons olive oil
- 2 tablespoons lemon juice

Method:
1. Take a skillet pan, place it over medium heat, add oil and when hot, add chickpeas, stir in salt and all the spices and cook for 3 minutes until warm.
2. When done, remove the pan from heat, sprinkle with sesame seeds and set aside.
3. Take a bowl, place all the ingredients for the salad in it, and toss until mixed.
4. Spread hummus on one side of the tortilla, top with chickpeas and salad, sprinkle with scallion, and then serve.

Nutrition Value:
- Calories: 405 Cal
- Fat: 16 g
- Carbs: 56.7 g
- Protein: 13.4 g
- Fiber: 12 g

Stuffed Peppers with Kidney Beans

Preparation time: 5 minutes
Cooking time: 35 minutes
Servings: 4

Ingredients:

- 3.5 ounces cooked kidney beans
- 1 big tomato, diced
- 3.5 ounces sweet corn, canned
- 2 medium bell peppers, deseeded, halved
- ½ of medium red onion, peeled, diced
- 1 teaspoon garlic powder
- 1/3 teaspoon ground black pepper
- 2/3 teaspoon salt
- ½ teaspoon dried basil
- 3 teaspoons parsley
- ½ teaspoon dried thyme
- 3 tablespoons cashew
- 1 teaspoon olive oil

Method:

1. Switch on the oven, then set it to 400 degrees F and let it preheat.
2. Take a large skillet pan, place it over medium heat, add oil and when hot, add onion and cook for 2 minutes until translucent.
3. Add beans, tomatoes, and corn, stir in garlic and cashews and cook for 5 minutes.
4. Stir in salt, black pepper, parsley, basil, and thyme, remove the pan from heat and evenly divide the mixture between bell peppers.
5. Bake the peppers for 25 minutes until tender, then top with parsley and serve.

Nutrition Value:

- Calories: 139 Cal
- Fat: 1.6 g
- Carbs: 18 g
- Protein: 5.1 g
- Fiber: 3.3 g

Thai Peanut Sauce over Roasted Sweet Potatoes

Preparation time: 10 minutes
Cooking time: 35 minutes
Servings: 4

Ingredients:

For the Thai Peanut Sauce:
- 1 teaspoon grated ginger
- 1 teaspoon garlic
- ¼ cup of soy sauce
- 3 tablespoons apple cider vinegar
- ¼ teaspoon red pepper flakes
- 2 tablespoons honey
- ½ cup peanut butter
- 2 tablespoons water

For the Roasted vegetables:
- 1 red bell pepper, cored, deseeded, sliced into strips
- 2 sweet potatoes, peeled, 1-inch
- 1 teaspoon salt
- ¼ teaspoon cumin powder
- 2 tablespoons olive oil

For the Garnish:
- 3 green onions, sliced
- 1 ¼ cup brown rice, cooked
- ½ cup cilantro
- ¼ cup peanuts, crushed

Method:

1. Prepare the vegetables and for this, place sweet potatoes on a baking sheet, drizzle with 1 tablespoon oil, season with ½ teaspoon salt and 1/8 teaspoon cumin, toss until mixed and roast for 35 minutes at 425 degrees F, tossing halfway.
2. In the meantime, place bell pepper strips on another baking sheet, drizzle with remaining oil, season with remaining salt, and toss until mixed and roast for 20 minutes at 425 degrees F, tossing halfway.
3. While vegetables are roasting, prepare the sauce and for this, place all its ingredients in a bowl and whisk until combined.
4. Distribute rice between four bowls, top with roasted vegetables, drizzle with sauce, garnish with peanuts, cilantro, and green onions, and serve.

Nutrition Value:
- Calories: 295 Cal
- Fat: 11.2 g
- Carbs: 38.8 g
- Protein: 9.8 g
- Fiber: 9.2 g

Beans Curry

Preparation time: 10 minutes
Cooking time: 8 hours and 10 minutes
Servings: 5

Ingredients:

- 2 cups kidney beans, dried, soaked
- 1-inch of ginger, grated
- 1 ½ cup diced tomatoes
- 1 medium red onion, peeled, sliced
- 1 tablespoon tomato paste
- 1 teaspoon minced garlic
- 1 small bunch cilantro, chopped
- ½ teaspoon cumin powder
- 1 teaspoon salt
- 1 ½ teaspoon curry powder
- 2 tablespoons olive oil
- 2 tablespoons lemon juice

Method:

1. Place onion in a food processor, add ginger and garlic, and pulse for 1 minute until blended.
2. Take a skillet pan, place it over medium heat, add oil and when hot, add the onion-garlic mixture, and cook for 5 minutes until softened and light brown.
3. Then add tomatoes and tomato paste, stir in ½ teaspoon salt, cumin and curry powder and cook for 5 minutes until cooked.
4. Drain the soaked beans, add them to the slow cooker, add cooked tomato mixture, and remaining ingredients except for cilantro and lemon juice and stir until mixed.
5. Switch on the slow cooker, then shut with lid and cook for 8 hours at high heat setting until tender.
6. When done, transfer 1 cup of beans to the blender, process until creamy, then return it into the slow cooker and stir until mixed.
7. Drizzle with lemon juice, top with cilantro, and serve.

Nutrition Value:

- Calories: 252 Cal
- Fat: 6.5 g
- Carbs: 38 g
- Protein: 13 g
- Fiber: 9.3 g

Ratatouille

Preparation time: 5 minutes
Cooking time: 15 minutes
Servings: 4

Ingredients:

- 2 medium zucchinis, sliced into ½-inch sliced moons
- 1 large eggplant, cut into ½-inch pieces
- 2 medium tomatoes, cut into ¾-inch wedges
- 1 red bell pepper, sliced into ½-inch strips
- 1 medium white onion, sliced
- 12 cloves of garlic, peeled
- 1 teaspoon salt
- 1 teaspoon balsamic vinegar
- 1/3 teaspoon ground black pepper
- 3 tablespoons rosemary and thyme
- Olive oil as needed

Method:

1. Prepare all the vegetables, then spread them in a single layer on a greased sheet pan, add garlic and herbs, drizzle with oil, toss until coated and season with salt with black pepper.
2. Toss the vegetables, roast them for 40 minutes at 400 degrees F, tossing halfway, and then continue roasting for 20 minutes at 300 degrees F until tender.
3. When done, taste to adjust salt, drizzle with vinegar and serve.

Nutrition Value:

- Calories: 147 Cal
- Fat: 9.7 g
- Carbs: 15.1 g
- Protein: 2.5 g
- Fiber: 4.2 g

Summer Minestrone

Preparation time: 5 minutes
Cooking time: 15 minutes
Servings: 4

Ingredients:

- 1 medium yellow squash, cut into 1/2-inch pieces
- 1/2 cup frozen peas
- 1 small carrot, peeled, sliced
- 1 small zucchini, cut into 1/2-inch pieces
- 8 ounces red potatoes, peeled, cut into 1/2-inch pieces
- 1 large onion, peeled, chopped
- 1 tablespoon olive oil
- 1 teaspoon minced garlic
- 1/3 teaspoon ground black pepper
- 2/3 teaspoon salt
- 1 cup chopped basil
- 4 cups vegetable broth
- 1/4 cup grated vegan parmesan cheese

Method:

1. Take a large saucepan, place it over medium heat, add oil and when hot, add onion, stir in black pepper and salt and cook for 8 minutes.
2. Then stir in garlic, cook for 1 minute, stir in potatoes, pour in broth and simmer for 5 minutes.
3. Add carrot, squash, and zucchini, continue simmer for 3 minutes, and then add peas, simmer for another 3 minutes.
4. Stir in basil and cheese and then serve with bread.

Nutrition Value:

- Calories: 185 Cal
- Fat: 6 g
- Carbs: 29 g
- Protein: 7 g
- Fiber: 5 g

Mushroom and Broccoli Noodles

Preparation time: 10 minutes
Cooking time: 10 minutes
Servings: 4

Ingredients:

- 2 linguine pasta, whole-grain, cooked
- 8 ounces chestnut mushroom, sliced
- 4 spring onions, sliced
- 1 small head of broccoli, cut into florets, steamed
- ½ teaspoon minced garlic
- ½ teaspoon red chili flakes
- 1 tablespoon sesame oil
- 2 teaspoons hoisin sauce
- ¼ cup roasted cashew
- 3 tablespoons stock

Method:

1. Take a large frying pan, place it over medium heat, add oil and when hot, add mushrooms and cook for 2 minutes until golden.
2. Stir in garlic, onion and chili flakes, cook for 1 minute, stir in broccoli and toss in pasta until hot.
3. Drizzle with hoisin sauce and 3 tablespoons of stock, toss until mixed, cook for 1 minute and remove the pan from heat.
4. Top with cashews, drizzle with some more sesame oil and serve.

Nutrition Value:

- Calories: 624 Cal
- Fat: 14 g
- Carbs: 105 g
- Protein: 25 g
- Fiber: 8 g

Balsamic-Glazed Roasted Cauliflower

Preparation time: 10 minutes
Cooking time: 1 hour and 5 minutes
Servings: 4

Ingredients:

- 1 large head cauliflower, cut into florets
- 1/2-pound green beans, trimmed
- 1 medium red onion, peeled, cut into wedges
- 2 cups cherry tomatoes
- ½ teaspoon salt
- 1/4 cup brown sugar
- 3 tablespoons olive oil
- 1 cup balsamic vinegar
- 2 tablespoons chopped parsley, for garnish

Method:

1. Place cauliflower florets in a baking dish, add tomatoes, green beans and onion wedges around it, season with salt, and drizzle with oil.
2. Pour vinegar in a saucepan, stir in sugar, bring the mixture to a boil and simmer for 15 minutes until reduced by half.
3. Brush the sauce generously over cauliflower florets and then roast for 1 hour at 400 degrees F until cooked, brushing sauce frequently.
4. When done, garnish vegetables with parsley and then serve.

Nutrition Value:

- Calories: 86 Cal
- Fat: 5.7 g
- Carbs: 7.7 g
- Protein: 3.1 g
- Fiber: 3.3 g

Pasta with Creamy Greens and Lemon

Preparation time: 5 minutes
Cooking time: 10 minutes
Servings: 4

Ingredients:

- 5 ounces broccoli, cut into florets
- 3.5 ounces frozen soya beans
- ¼ cup basil leaves
- 3.5 ounces frozen peas
- 3.5 ounces mange tout
- 2/3 teaspoon salt
- 1/3 teaspoon ground black pepper
- 1 lemon, juiced, zested
- 5.3 ounces vegan mascarpone
- 3 ounces grated vegan parmesan cheese
- 12 ounces whole-grain pasta, cooked

Method:

1. Cook the pasta in a saucepan, add all the vegetables in the last 3 minutes, and, when done, drain the pasta and vegetables.
2. Return the pasta and vegetables into the pan, add remaining ingredients and stir until well combined.
3. Serve straight away.

Nutrition Value:

- Calories: 635 Cal
- Fat: 28 g
- Carbs: 75 g
- Protein: 26 g
- Fiber: 7 g

Blackened Tempeh

Preparation time: 10 minutes
Cooking time: 10 minutes
Servings: 2

Ingredients:

For the Ranch Dressing:
- 1 teaspoon Cajun spice blend

For the Blackened Tempeh:
- 4 radishes, sliced
- 3 cups shredded kale
- 1 medium avocado, pitted, sliced
- 1 block of tempeh
- 3 tablespoons Cajun Spice
- ½ a lemon, zested
- 1/3 cup vegan ranch dressing
- ¼ cup pickled onions
- ¼ teaspoon salt
- 1 teaspoon peanut oil
- 2 tablespoons olive oil
- 1 scallion, sliced

Method:

1. Prepare the ranch dressing and for this, place all its ingredients in a bowl and stir until combined, set aside until required.
2. Take a sauté pan, place it over medium heat, add tempeh, pour in salted water to cover it, and simmer for 8 minutes until its bitterness has reduced.
3. When done, transfer tempeh to a cutting board, then cut it ½-inch slices and season with Cajun spices until coated on both sides.
4. Place shredded kale in a bowl, drizzle with peanut oil, season with salt and lemon zest, massage with fingers, then add remaining ingredients along with ranch dressing and toss until coated.
5. Distribute the kale salad between the bowl, top with tempeh and scallions and then serve.

Nutrition Value:
- Calories: 281 Cal
- Fat: 18.1 g
- Carbs: 17.1 g
- Protein: 17 g
- Fiber: 11.4 g

Avocado Linguine

Preparation time: 10 minutes
Cooking time: 0 minute
Servings: 4

Ingredients:

- ½ cup arugula
- 2 medium avocados
- 2 cloves of garlic, peeled
- 1/4 teaspoon ground white pepper
- 3/4 teaspoons salt
- 1 teaspoon lemon zest
- 3 tablespoons lemon juice
- 3 tablespoons olive oil
- 8 ounces linguine, whole-wheat, boiled

Method:

1. Prepare the avocado sauce, and for this, place all the ingredients in a food processor, except for pasta, arugula, pepper, and lemon zest and pulse until smooth.
2. Tip the puree in a large bowl, add remaining ingredients, toss until well mixed and taste to adjust seasoning.
3. Serve straight away.

Nutrition Value:

- Calories: 387 Cal
- Fat: 16.6 g
- Carbs: 54.3 g
- Protein: 9.4 g
- Fiber: 8.6 g

Tomato and Basil Sauce

Preparation time: 5 minutes
Cooking time: 10 minutes
Servings: 4

Ingredients:

- 14 ounces chopped tomatoes
- ½ teaspoon minced garlic
- 1 teaspoon vegetable stock powder
- 1 teaspoon sugar
- 1 tablespoon tomato purée
- 5 basil leaves
- 1 tablespoon olive oil
- ¼ cup vegetable stock

Method:

1. Take a skillet pan, place it over medium heat, add oil and when hot, add garlic and cook for 1 minute until fragrant.
2. Then stir in tomatoes and remaining ingredients until combined, except for basil, and bring the mixture to boil.
3. Switch heat to the low level, simmer the mixture for 5 minutes, and when done, top with basil.
4. Serve straight away.

Nutrition Value:

- Calories: 52 Cal
- Fat: 3 g
- Carbs: 5 g
- Protein: 2 g
- Fiber: 1 g

Zaatar Roasted Eggplant

Preparation time: 10 minutes
Cooking time: 60 minutes
Servings: 2

Ingredients:

- 1-pound eggplant, destemmed
- ½ teaspoon minced garlic
- ¼ teaspoon salt
- 1 tablespoon zaatar spice mix
- 1 ½ tablespoon olive oil

For Serving:

- 2 cups chopped tomatoes
- 2 cups cooked brown rice
- Tahini sauce as needed
- Parsley for serving

Method:

1. Prepare the eggplant, and for this, cut it into half, then make deep diagonals in it at 1-inch interval, but not cutting through the skin and season with 1/8 teaspoon salt.
2. Place remaining ingredients in a bowl, stir until the smooth paste comes together, then brush it well on the eggplant, bake for 1 hour until tender, rotating halfway, and when done, pierce it with a fork.
3. When done, top eggplant with rice and tomatoes, drizzle with tahini sauce, top with parsley and serve.

Nutrition Value:

- Calories: 268 Cal
- Fat: 12 g
- Carbs: 32 g
- Protein: 8 g
- Fiber: 12 g

Butternut Squash Linguine

Preparation time: 10 minutes
Cooking time: 35 minutes
Servings: 4

Ingredients:

- 1 medium white onion, peeled, chopped
- 3 cups diced butternut squash, peeled, deseeded
- 1 teaspoon minced garlic
- ½ teaspoon salt
- ⅛ teaspoon red pepper flakes
- ¼ teaspoon ground black pepper
- 1 tablespoon chopped sage
- 2 tablespoons olive oil
- 2 cups vegetable broth
- 12 ounces linguine, whole-grain, cooked

Method:

1. Take a large skillet pan, place it over medium heat, add oil and when hot, add sage and cook for 3 minutes until crispy.
2. Transfer sage to a bowl, sprinkle with some salt and set aside until required.
3. Add onion, squash pieces, and garlic into the pan, season with salt, red pepper and black pepper, stir until mixed and cook for 10 minutes.
4. Pour in broth, stir, bring the mixture to boil, then switch heat to medium-low level and simmer for 20 minutes.
5. When done, remove the pan from heat, puree by using an immersion blender until smooth, taste to adjust seasoning and return it into the pan.
6. Heat the pan over medium heat, add cooked pasta, toss until well coated and cook for 2 minutes until hot.
7. Serve straight away.

Nutrition Value:

- Calories: 380 Cal
- Fat: 9 g
- Carbs: 68.4 g
- Protein: 10.7 g
- Fiber: 10.8 g

Vegetarian fajitas

Preparation time: 10 minutes
Cooking time: 15 minutes
Servings: 6

Ingredients:

For the Vegetables:
- 12 ounces cooked black beans
- 1 yellow bell pepper, cored, sliced
- 2 green bell peppers, cored, sliced
- 1 medium-sized white onion, peeled, sliced
- 1 red bell pepper, cored, sliced
- 3 tablespoons olive oil

For the Fajita Seasoning:
- 1/2 teaspoon onion powder
- 1/2 teaspoon garlic powder
- 1/2 teaspoon ground black pepper
- 1/2 teaspoon salt
- 2 teaspoons red chili powder
- 1/8 teaspoon cayenne pepper
- 1 teaspoon paprika

For the Toppings:
- 6 small tortillas
- Guacamole as needed
- 1 lime, cut into wedges
- 2 tablespoons chopped cilantro

Method:

1. Prepare the fajita seasoning and for this, stir all its ingredients, then sprinkle with over onion and bell peppers, drizzle with oil, toss until well coated, spread them evenly on a sheet pan and bake for 15 minutes until roasted, tossing halfway.
2. When done, heat beans over low heat until hot, then distribute it evenly on the tortilla, top with roasted vegetables, guacamole, and cilantro and serve with lime wedges.

Nutrition Value:
- Calories: 288 Cal
- Fat: 6.7 g
- Carbs: 49 g
- Protein: 10.1 g
- Fiber: 11 g

Spiced Carrot and Lentil Soup

Preparation time: 5 minutes
Cooking time: 20 minutes
Servings: 4

Ingredients:

- 22 ounces carrots, grated
- 5 ounces split red lentils
- ½ teaspoon salt
- 2 teaspoons cumin seeds, toasted
- 1/8 teaspoon red chili flakes
- 2 tablespoons olive oil
- 4 cups vegetable stock, hot
- ½ cup of coconut milk

Method:

1. Take a large saucepan, add 1 teaspoon cumin seeds, half of the red chili flakes along with remaining ingredients, stir until combined, and bring the mixture to a boil over medium-high heat.
2. Switch heat to medium level, simmer for 15 minutes until lentils have softened, and when done, puree the soup by using an immersion blender until smooth.
3. Serve straight away.

Nutrition Value:

- Calories: 238 Cal
- Fat: 7 g
- Carbs: 34 g
- Protein: 11 g
- Fiber: 5 g

Chapter 7: Snack and Sides

Zucchini Chips

Preparation time: 10 minutes
Cooking time: 120 minutes
Servings: 4

Ingredients:
- 1 large zucchini, thinly sliced
- 1 teaspoon salt
- 2 tablespoons olive oil

Method:
1. Pat dry zucchini slices and then spread them in an even layer on a baking sheet lined with parchment sheet.
2. Whisk together salt and oil, brush this mixture over zucchini slices on both sides and then bake for 2 hours or more until brown and crispy.
3. When done, let the chips cool for 10 minutes and then serve straight away.

Nutrition Value:
- Calories: 54 Cal
- Fat: 5 g
- Carbs: 1 g
- Protein: 0 g
- Fiber: 0.3 g

Pumpkin Cake Pops

Preparation time: 10 minutes
Cooking time: 10 minutes
Servings: 4

Ingredients:

- 1 cup coconut flour
- ¼ teaspoon cinnamon
- 1/4 cup coconut sugar
- 1/4 cup chocolate chips, unsweetened
- 3/4 cup pumpkin puree

Method:

1. Place all the ingredients in a bowl, except for chocolate chips, stir until incorporated, and then fold in chocolate chips until combined.
2. Shape the mixture into small balls, then place them on a cookie sheet greased with oil and bake for 10 minutes at 350 degrees F until done.
3. Let the balls cool completely and then serve.

Nutrition Value:

- Calories: 82.5 Cal
- Fat: 3.4 g
- Carbs: 12.3 g
- Protein: 0.7 g
- Fiber: 0.05 g

Cinnamon Bananas

Preparation time: 5 minutes
Cooking time: 8 minutes
Servings: 2

Ingredients:

- 2 bananas, peeled, sliced
- 1 teaspoon cinnamon
- 2 tablespoons granulated Splenda
- 1/4 teaspoon nutmeg

Method:

1. Prepare the cinnamon mixture and for this, place all the ingredients in a bowl, except for banana, and stir until mixed.
2. Take a large skillet pan, place it over medium heat, spray with oil, add banana slices and sprinkle with half of the prepared cinnamon mixture.
3. Cook for 3 minutes, then sprinkle with remaining prepared cinnamon mixture and continue cooking for 3 minutes until tender and hot.
4. Serve straight away.

Nutrition Value:

- Calories: 155 Cal
- Fat: 2 g
- Carbs: 39 g
- Protein: 1 g
- Fiber: 3 g

Oven-Dried Grapes

Preparation time: 5 minutes
Cooking time: 4 hours
Servings: 4

Ingredients:

- 3 large bunches of grapes, seedless
- Olive oil as needed for greasing

Method:

1. Spread grapes into two greased baking sheets and bake for 4 hours at 225 degrees F until semi-dried.
2. When done, let the grape cool completely and then serve.

Nutrition Value:

- Calories: 299 Cal
- Fat: 1 g
- Carbs: 79 g
- Protein: 3.1 g
- Fiber: 3.7 g

Beans and Spinach Tacos

Preparation time: 10 minutes
Cooking time: 15 minutes
Servings: 4

Ingredients:

- 12 ounces spinach
- 4 tablespoons cooked kidney beans
- ½ of medium red onion, peeled, chopped
- ½ teaspoon minced garlic
- 1 medium tomato, chopped
- 3 tablespoons chopped parsley
- ½ of avocado, sliced
- ½ teaspoon ground black pepper
- 1 teaspoon salt
- 2 tablespoons olive oil
- 4 slices of vegan brie cheese
- 4 tortillas, about 6-inches

Method:

1. Take a skillet pan, place it over medium heat, add oil and when hot, add onion and cook for 10 minutes until softened.
2. Then stir in spinach, cook for 4 minutes until its leaves wilts, then drain it and distribute evenly between tortillas.
3. Top evenly with remaining ingredients, season with black pepper and salt, drizzle with lemon juice and then serve.

Nutrition Value:

- Calories: 219.8 Cal
- Fat: 6 g
- Carbs: 34 g
- Protein: 9.9 g
- Fiber: 10 g

Black Bean Lime Dip

Preparation time: 5 minutes
Cooking time: 6 minutes
Servings: 4

Ingredients:

- 15.5 ounces cooked black beans
- 1 teaspoon minced garlic
- ½ of a lime, juiced
- 1 inch of ginger, grated
- 1/3 teaspoon salt
- 1/3 teaspoon ground black pepper
- 1 tablespoon olive oil

Method:

1. Take a frying pan, add oil and when hot, add garlic and ginger and cook for 1 minute until fragrant.
2. Then add beans, splash with some water and fry for 3 minutes until hot.
3. Season beans with salt and black pepper, drizzle with lime juice, then remove the pan from heat and mash the beans until smooth pasta comes together.
4. Serve the dip with whole-grain breadsticks or vegetables.

Nutrition Value:

- Calories: 374 Cal
- Fat: 14 g
- Carbs: 46 g
- Protein: 15 g
- Fiber: 17 g

Watermelon Pizza

Preparation time: 10 minutes
Cooking time: 0 minute
Servings: 10

Ingredients:

- 1/2 cup strawberries, halved
- 1/2 cup blueberries
- 1 watermelon
- 1/2 cup raspberries
- 1 cup of coconut yogurt
- 1/2 cup pomegranate seeds
- 1/2 cup cherries
- Maple syrup as needed

Method:

1. Cut watermelon into 3-inch thick slices, then spread yogurt on one side, leaving some space in the edges and then top evenly with fruits and drizzle with maple syrup.
2. Cut the watermelon into wedges and then serve.

Nutrition Value:

- Calories: 150 Cal
- Fat: 4 g
- Carbs: 21 g
- Protein: 10 g
- Fiber: 2 g

Zucchini and Amaranth Patties

Preparation time: 10 minutes

Cooking time: 30 minutes

Servings: 14

Ingredients:

- 1 1/2 cups shredded zucchini
- ½ of a medium onion, shredded
- 1 1/2 cups cooked white beans
- 1/2 cup amaranth seeds
- 1 teaspoon red chili powder
- 1/2 teaspoon cumin
- 1/2 cup cornmeal
- 1/4 cup flax meal
- 1 tablespoon salsa
- 1 1/2 cups vegetable broth

Method:

1. Stir together stock and amaranth on a pot, bring it to a boil over medium-high heat, then switch heat to medium-low level and simmer until all the liquid is absorbed.
2. Mash the white beans in a bowl, add remaining ingredients including cooked amaranth and stir until well mixed.
3. Shape the mixture into patties, then place them on a baking sheet lined with parchment sheet and bake for 30 minutes until browned and crispy, turning halfway.
4. Serve straight away.

Nutrition Value:

- Calories: 152 Cal
- Fat: 3 g
- Carbs: 29 g
- Protein: 7 g
- Fiber: 6 g

Rice Pizza

Preparation time: 10 minutes
Cooking time: 35 minutes
Servings: 6

Ingredients:

For the Crust:
- 1 1/2 cup short-grain rice, cooked
- 1/2 teaspoon garlic powder
- 1 teaspoon coconut sugar
- 1 tablespoon red chili flakes

For the Sauce:
- 1/4 teaspoon onion powder
- 1 tablespoon nutritional yeast
- 1/4 teaspoon garlic powder
- 1/4 teaspoon ginger powder
- 1 tablespoon red chili flakes
- 1 teaspoon soy sauce
- 1/2 cup tomato purée

For the Toppings:
- 2 1/2 cups oyster mushrooms
- 1 chili pepper, deseeded, sliced
- 2 scallions, sliced
- 1 teaspoon coconut sugar
- 1 teaspoon soy sauce
- Baby corn as needed

Method:

1. Prepare the crust and for this, place all of its ingredients in a bowl and stir until well combined.
2. Then take a pizza pan, line it with parchment sheet, place rice mixture in it, spread it evenly, and then bake for 20 minutes at 350 degrees F.
3. Then spread tomato sauce over the crust, top evenly with remaining ingredients for the topping and continue baking for 15 minutes.
4. When done, slice the pizza into wedges and serve.

Nutrition Value:
- Calories: 140.1 Cal
- Fat: 5 g
- Carbs: 30 g
- Protein: 3 g
- Fiber: 1 g

Applesauce

Preparation time: 10 minutes
Cooking time: 15 minutes
Servings: 6

Ingredients:

- 4 pounds mixed apples, cored, ½-inch chopped
- 1 strip of orange peel, about 3-inch
- 1/2 cup coconut sugar
- 1/2 teaspoon salt
- 1 cinnamon stick, about 3-inch
- 2 tablespoons apple cider vinegar
- Apple cider as needed for consistency of the sauce

Method:

1. Take a large pot, place apples in it, then add remaining ingredients except for cider, stir until mixed and cook for 15 minutes over medium heat until apples have wilted, stirring every 10 minutes.
2. When done, remove the cinnamon stick and orange peel and puree the mixture by using an immersion blender until smooth and stir in apple cider until sauce reaches to desired consistency.
3. Serve straight away.

Nutrition Value:

- Calories: 75 Cal
- Fat: 0.2 g
- Carbs: 19 g
- Protein: 0.2 g
- Fiber: 1.3 g

Quinoa and Black Bean Burgers

Preparation time: 10 minutes
Cooking time: 6 minutes
Servings: 5

Ingredients:
- 1/4 cup quinoa, cooked
- 15 ounces cooked black beans
- 2 tablespoons minced white onion
- 1/4 cup minced bell pepper
- ½ teaspoon minced garlic
- 1/2 teaspoon salt
- 1 1/2 teaspoons ground cumin
- 1/2 cup bread crumbs
- 1 teaspoon hot pepper sauce
- 3 tablespoons olive oil
- 1 flax egg

Method:
1. Place all the ingredients in a bowl, except for oil, stir until well combined, and then shape the mixture into five patties.
2. Heat oil in a frying pan over medium heat, add patties and cook for 3 minutes per side until browned.
3. Serve straight away.

Nutrition Value:
- Calories: 245 Cal
- Fat: 10.6 g
- Carbs: 29 g
- Protein: 9.3 g
- Fiber: 7.2 g

Loaded Baked Potatoes

Preparation time: 10 minutes
Cooking time: 32 minutes
Servings: 2

Ingredients:

- 1/2 cup cooked chickpeas
- 2 medium potatoes, scrubbed
- 1 cup broccoli florets, steamed
- 1/4 cup vegan bacon bits
- 2 tablespoons all-purpose seasoning
- ¼ cup vegan cheese sauce
- 1/2 cup vegan sour cream

Method:

1. Pierce hole in the potatoes, microwave them for 12 minutes over high heat setting until soft to touch, and then bake them for 20 minutes at 450 degrees F until very tender.
2. Open the potatoes, mash the flesh with a fork, then top evenly with remaining ingredients and serve.

Nutrition Value:

- Calories: 422 Cal
- Fat: 16 g
- Carbs: 59 g
- Protein: 9 g
- Fiber: 6 g

Chapter 8: Desserts

Cookie Dough Bites

Preparation time: 4 hours and 10 minutes
Cooking time: 0 minute
Servings: 18

Ingredients:

- 15 ounces cooked chickpeas
- 1/3 cup vegan chocolate chips
- 1/3 cup and 2 tablespoons peanut butter
- 8 Medjool dates pitted
- 1 teaspoon vanilla extract, unsweetened
- 2 tablespoons maple syrup
- 1 1/2 tablespoons almond milk, unsweetened

Method:

1. Place chickpeas in a food processor along with dates, butter, and vanilla and then process for 2 minutes until smooth.
2. Add remaining ingredients, except for chocolate chips, and then pulse for 1 minute until blends and dough comes together.
3. Add chocolate chips, stir until just mixed, then shape the mixture into 18 balls and refrigerate for 4 hours until firm.
4. Serve straight away

Nutrition Value:

- Calories: 200 Cal
- Fat: 9 g
- Carbs: 26 g
- Protein: 1 g
- Fiber: 0 g

Coconut Lemon Tart

Preparation time: 3 hours and 15 minutes
Cooking time: 10 minutes
Servings: 8

Ingredients:

For the Crust:
- 1/2 cup shredded coconut, unsweetened
- 1/2 cup almonds
- 1/2 cup pecans
- 1/2 cup dates

For the Filling:
- 1/2 tablespoon lemon zest
- 2 tablespoons cornstarch
- 1/2 cup agave nectar
- 1 1/2 cups and 2 tablespoons lemon juice
- 1/2 teaspoon agar powder
- 7.5 ounces coconut cream
- 1/4 cup water

Method:

1. Prepare the crust, and for this, place all its ingredients in a food processor and pulse for 3 to 5 minutes until the thick paste comes together.
2. Take a 10-inch pie pan, dust it lightly with coconut, pour crust mixture in it and spread and press the mixture evenly in the bottom and sides, and freeze until required.
3. Prepare the filling and for this, place a saucepan, place it over medium-low heat, add all the ingredients of filling, and whisk well and simmer for 10 minutes until the filling has thickened, whisking constantly.
4. Let filling cool for 5 minutes, pour the filling into the prepared tart, smooth the top and freeze for 3 hours until set.
5. Cut tart into slices and then serve.

Nutrition Value:
- Calories: 249 Cal
- Fat: 15 g
- Carbs: 28 g
- Protein: 2.8 g
- Fiber: 1 g

Strawberry Coconut Ice Cream

Preparation time: 5 minutes
Cooking time: 0 minute
Servings: 4

Ingredients:
- 4 cups frouncesen strawberries
- 1 vanilla bean, seeded
- 28 ounces coconut cream
- 1/2 cup maple syrup

Method:
1. Place cream in a food processor and pulse for 1 minute until soft peaks come together.
2. Then tip the cream in a bowl, add remaining ingredients in the blender and blend until thick mixture comes together.
3. Add the mixture into the cream, fold until combined, and then transfer ice cream into a freezer-safe bowl and freeze for 4 hours until firm, whisking every 20 minutes after 1 hour.
4. Serve straight away.

Nutrition Value:
- Calories: 100 Cal
- Fat: 100 g
- Carbs: 100 g
- Protein: 100 g
- Fiber: 100 g

Chocolate and Avocado Truffles

Preparation time: 1 hour and 10 minutes
Cooking time: 1 minute
Servings: 18

Ingredients:

- 1 medium avocado, ripe
- 2 tablespoons cocoa powder
- 10 ounces of dark chocolate chips

Method:

1. Scoop out the flesh from avocado, place it in a bowl, then mash with a fork until smooth, and stir in 1/2 cup chocolate chips.
2. Place remaining chocolate chips in a heatproof bowl and microwave for 1 minute until chocolate has melted, stirring halfway.
3. Add melted chocolate into avocado mixture, stir well until blended, and then refrigerate for 1 hour.
4. Then shape the mixture into balls, 1 tablespoon of mixture per ball, and roll in cocoa powder until covered.
5. Serve straight away.

Nutrition Value:

- Calories: 59 Cal
- Fat: 4 g
- Carbs: 7 g
- Protein: 0 g
- Fiber: 1 g

Chocolate Avocado Ice Cream

Preparation time: 1 hour and 10 minutes
Cooking time: 0 minute
Servings: 2

Ingredients:

- 4.5 ounces avocado, peeled, pitted
- 1/2 cup cocoa powder, unsweetened
- 1 tablespoon vanilla extract, unsweetened
- 1/2 cup and 2 tablespoons maple syrup
- 13.5 ounces coconut milk, unsweetened
- 1/2 cup water

Method:

1. Add avocado in a food processor along with milk and then pulse for 2 minutes until smooth.
2. Add remaining ingredients, blend until mixed, and then tip the pudding in a freezer-proof container.
3. Place the container in a freezer and chill for freeze for 4 hours until firm, whisking every 20 minutes after 1 hour.
4. Serve straight away.

Nutrition Value:

- Calories: 80.7 Cal
- Fat: 7.1 g
- Carbs: 6 g
- Protein: 0.6 g
- Fiber: 2 g

Chocolate Peanut Butter Energy Bites

Preparation time: 1 hour and 5 minutes
Cooking time: 0 minute
Servings: 4

Ingredients:

- 1/2 cup oats, old-fashioned
- 1/3 cup cocoa powder, unsweetened
- 1 cup dates, chopped
- 1/2 cup shredded coconut flakes, unsweetened
- 1/2 cup peanut butter

Method:

1. Place oats in a food processor along with dates and pulse for 1 minute until the paste starts to come together.
2. Then add remaining ingredients, and blend until incorporated and very thick mixture comes together.
3. Shape the mixture into balls, refrigerate for 1 hour until set and then serve.

Nutrition Value:

- Calories: 88.6 Cal
- Fat: 5 g
- Carbs: 10 g
- Protein: 2.3 g
- Fiber: 1.6 g

Dark Chocolate Raspberry Ice Cream

Preparation time: 5 minutes
Cooking time: 0 minute
Servings: 2

Ingredients:
- 2 frouncesen bananas, sliced
- ¼ cup fresh raspberries
- 2 tablespoons cocoa powder, unsweetened
- 2 tablespoons raspberry jelly

Method:
1. Place all the ingredients in a food processor, except for berries and pulse for 2 minutes until smooth.
2. Distribute the ice cream mixture between two bowls, stir in berries until combined, and then serve immediately.

Nutrition Value:
- Calories: 104 Cal
- Fat: 0 g
- Carbs: 25 g
- Protein: 0 g
- Fiber: 5 g

Strawberry Mousse

Preparation time: 5 minutes
Cooking time: 15 minutes
Servings: 4

Ingredients:

- 8 ounces coconut milk, unsweetened
- 2 tablespoons honey
- 5 strawberries

Method:

1. Place berries in a blender and pulse until the smooth mixture comes together.
2. Place milk in a bowl, whisk until whipped, and then add remaining ingredients and stir until combined.
3. Refrigerate the mousse for 10 minutes and then serve.

Nutrition Value:

- Calories: 145 Cal
- Fat: 23 g
- Carbs: 15 g
- Protein: 5 g
- Fiber: 1 g

Brownie Batter

Preparation time: 5 minutes
Cooking time: 0 minute
Servings: 4

Ingredients:

- 4 Medjool dates, pitted, soaked in warm water
- 1.5 ounces chocolate, unsweetened, melted
- 2 tablespoons maple syrup
- 4 tablespoons tahini
- ½ teaspoon vanilla extract, unsweetened
- 1 tablespoon cocoa powder, unsweetened
- 1/8 teaspoon sea salt
- 1/8 teaspoon espresso powder
- 2 to 4 tablespoons almond milk, unsweetened

Method:

1. Place all the ingredients in a food processor and process for 2 minutes until combined.
2. Set aside until required.

Nutrition Value:

- Calories: 44 Cal
- Fat: 1 g
- Carbs: 6 g
- Protein: 2 g
- Fiber: 0 g

Peanut Butter Energy Bars

Preparation time: 5 hours and 15 minutes
Cooking time: 5 minutes
Servings: 16

Ingredients:

- 1/2 cup cranberries
- 12 Medjool dates, pitted
- 1 cup roasted almond
- 1 tablespoon chia seeds
- 1 1/2 cups oats
- 1/8 teaspoon salt
- 1/4 cup and 1 tablespoon agave nectar
- 1/2 teaspoon vanilla extract, unsweetened
- 1/3 cup and 1 tablespoon peanut butter, unsalted
- 2 tablespoons water

Method:

1. Place an almond in a food processor, pulse until chopped, and then transfer into a large bowl.
2. Add dates into the food processor along with oats, pour in water, and pulse for dates are chopped.
3. Add dates mixture into the almond mixture, add chia seeds and berries and stir until mixed.
4. Take a saucepan, place it over medium heat, add remaining butter and remaining ingredients, stir and cook for 5 minutes until mixture reaches to a liquid consistency.
5. Pour the butter mixture over date mixture, and then stir until well combined.
6. Take an 8 by 8 inches baking tray, line it with parchment sheet, add date mixture in it, spread and press it evenly and refrigerate for 5 hours.
7. Cut it into sixteen bars and serve.

Nutrition Value:

- Calories: 187 Cal
- Fat: 7.5 g
- Carbs: 27.2 g
- Protein: 4.7 g
- Fiber: 2 g

Mango Coconut Cheesecake

Preparation time: 4 hours and 10 minutes
Cooking time: 0 minute
Servings: 4

Ingredients:

For the Crust:
- 1 cup macadamia nuts
- 1 cup dates, pitted, soaked in hot water for 10 minutes

For the Filling:
- 2 cups cashews, soaked in warm water for 10 minutes
- 1/2 cup and 1 tablespoon maple syrup
- 1/3 cup and 2 tablespoons coconut oil
- 1/4 cup lemon juice
- 1/2 cup and 2 tablespoons coconut milk, unsweetened, chilled

For the Topping:
- 1 cup fresh mango slices

Method:
1. Prepare the crust, and for this, place nuts in a food processor and process until mixture resembles crumbs.
2. Drain the dates, add them to the food processor and blend for 2 minutes until thick mixture comes together.
3. Take a 4-inch cheesecake pan, place date mixture in it, spread and press evenly, and set aside.
4. Prepare the filling and for this, place all its ingredients in a food processor and blend for 3 minutes until smooth.
5. Pour the filling into the crust, spread evenly, and then freeze for 4 hours until set.
6. Top the cake with mango slices and then serve.

Nutrition Value:
- Calories: 200 Cal
- Fat: 11 g
- Carbs: 22.5 g
- Protein: 2 g
- Fiber: 1 g

Chocolate Mint Grasshopper Pie

Preparation time: 4 hours and 15 minutes
Cooking time: 0 minute
Servings: 4

Ingredients:

For the Crust:
- 1 cup dates, soaked in warm water for 10 minutes in water, drained
- 1/8 teaspoons salt
- 1/2 cup pecans
- 1 teaspoons cinnamon
- 1/2 cup walnuts

For the Filling:
- ½ cup mint leaves
- 2 cups of cashews, soaked in warm water for 10 minutes in water, drained
- 2 tablespoons coconut oil
- 1/4 cup and 2 tablespoons of agave
- 1/4 teaspoons spirulina
- 1/4 cup water

Method:

1. Prepare the crust, and for this, place all its ingredients in a food processor and pulse for 3 to 5 minutes until the thick paste comes together.
2. Take a 6-inch springform pan, grease it with oil, place crust mixture in it and spread and press the mixture evenly in the bottom and along the sides, and freeze until required.
3. Prepare the filling and for this, place all its ingredients in a food processor, and pulse for 2 minutes until smooth.
4. Pour the filling into prepared pan, smooth the top, and freeze for 4 hours until set.
5. Cut pie into slices and then serve.

Nutrition Value:
- Calories: 223.7 Cal
- Fat: 7.5 g
- Carbs: 36 g
- Protein: 2.5 g
- Fiber: 1 g

Lemon Cashew Tart

Preparation time: 3 hours and 15 minutes
Cooking time: 0 minute
Servings: 12

Ingredients:

For the Crust:
- 1 cup almonds
- 4 dates, pitted, soaked in warm water for 10 minutes in water, drained
- 1/8 teaspoon crystal salt
- 1 teaspoon vanilla extract, unsweetened

For the Cream:
- 1 cup cashews, soaked in warm water for 10 minutes in water, drained
- 1/4 cup water
- 1/4 cup coconut nectar
- 1 teaspoon coconut oil
- 1 teaspoon vanilla extract, unsweetened
- 1 lemon, Juiced
- 1/8 teaspoon crystal salt

For the Topping:
- Shredded coconut as needed

Method:
1. Prepare the cream and for this, place all its ingredients in a food processor, pulse for 2 minutes until smooth, and then refrigerate for 1 hour.
2. Then prepare the crust, and for this, place all its ingredients in a food processor and pulse for 3 to 5 minutes until the thick paste comes together.
3. Take a tart pan, grease it with oil, place crust mixture in it and spread and press the mixture evenly in the bottom and along the sides, and freeze until required.
4. Pour the filling into the prepared tart, smooth the top, and refrigerate for 2 hours until set.
5. Cut tart into slices and then serve.

Nutrition Value:
- Calories: 166 Cal
- Fat: 10 g
- Carbs: 15 g
- Protein: 5 g
- Fiber: 1 g

Matcha Coconut Cream Pie

Preparation time: 5 minutes
Cooking time: 0 minute
Servings: 4

Ingredients:

For the Crust:
- 1/2 cup ground flaxseed
- 3/4 cup shredded dried coconut
- 1 cup Medjool dates, pitted
- 3/4 cup dehydrated buckwheat groats
- 1/4 teaspoons sea salt

For the Filling:
- 1 cup dried coconut flakes
- 4 cups of coconut meat
- 1/4 cup and 2 Tablespoons coconut nectar
- 1/2 Tablespoons vanilla extract, unsweetened
- 1/4 teaspoons sea salt
- 2/3 cup and 2 Tablespoons coconut butter
- 1 Tablespoons matcha powder
- 1/2 cup coconut water

Method:

1. Prepare the crust, and for this, place all its ingredients in a food processor and pulse for 3 to 5 minutes until the thick paste comes together.
2. Take a 6-inch springform pan, grease it with oil, place crust mixture in it and spread and press the mixture evenly in the bottom and along the sides, and freeze until required.
3. Prepare the filling and for this, place all its ingredients in a food processor, and pulse for 2 minutes until smooth.
4. Pour the filling into prepared pan, smooth the top, and freeze for 4 hours until set.
5. Cut pie into slices and then serve.

Nutrition Value:
- Calories: 209 Cal
- Fat: 18 g
- Carbs: 10 g
- Protein: 1 g
- Fiber: 2 g

Chapter 9: Homemade Basics, Sauces, and Condiments

Tomato Jam

Preparation time: 10 minutes
 Cooking time: 20 minutes
 Servings: 16

Ingredients:

- 2 pounds tomatoes
- ¼ teaspoon. ground black pepper
- ½ teaspoon. salt
- ¼ cup coconut sugar
- ½ teaspoon. white wine vinegar
- ¼ teaspoon. smoked paprika

Method:

1. Place a large pot filled with water over medium heat, bring it to boil, then add tomatoes and boil for 1 minute.
2. Transfer tomatoes to a bowl containing chilled water, let them stand for 2 minutes, and then peel them by hand.
3. Cut the tomatoes, remove and discard seeds, then chop tomatoes and place them in a large pot.
4. Sprinkle sugar over coconut, stir until mixed and let it stand for 10 minutes.
5. Then place the pot over medium-high heat, cook for 15 minutes, then add remaining ingredients except for vinegar and cook for 10 minutes until thickened.
6. Remove pot from heat, stir in vinegar and serve.

Nutrition Value:

- Calories: 17.6 Cal
- Fat: 1.3 g
- Carbs: 1.5 g
- Protein: 0.2 g
- Fiber: 0.3 g

Green Goddess Hummus

Preparation time: 5 minutes
Cooking time: 0 minute
Servings: 6

Ingredients:

- ¼ cup tahini
- ¼ cup lemon juice
- 2 tablespoons olive oil
- ½ cup chopped parsley
- ¼ cup chopped basil
- 3 tablespoons chopped chives
- 1 large clove of garlic, peeled, chopped
- ½ teaspoon salt
- 15-ounce cooked chickpeas
- 2 tablespoons water

Method:

1. Place all the ingredients in the order in a food processor or blender and then pulse for 3 to 5 minutes at high speed until the thick mixture comes together.
2. Tip the hummus in a bowl and then serve.

Nutrition Value:

- Calories: 110.4 Cal
- Fat: 6 g
- Carbs: 11.5 g
- Protein: 4.8 g
- Fiber: 2.6 g

Barbecue Tahini Sauce

Preparation time: 5 minutes
Cooking time: 0 minute
Servings: 8

Ingredients:

- 6 tablespoons tahini
- 3/4 teaspoon garlic powder
- 1/8 teaspoon red chili powder
- 2 teaspoons maple syrup
- 1/4 teaspoon salt
- 3 teaspoons molasses
- 3 teaspoons apple cider vinegar
- 1/4 teaspoon liquid smoke
- 10 teaspoons tomato paste
- 1/2 cup water

Method:

1. Place all the ingredients in the order in a food processor or blender and then pulse for 3 to 5 minutes at high speed until smooth.
2. Tip the sauce in a bowl and then serve.

Nutrition Value:

- Calories: 86 Cal
- Fat: 5 g
- Carbs: 7 g
- Protein: 2 g
- Fiber: 0 g

Spicy Red Wine Tomato Sauce

Preparation time: 5 minutes

Cooking time: 1 hour

Servings: 4

Ingredients:

- 28 ounces puree of whole tomatoes, peeled
- 4 cloves of garlic, peeled
- 1 tablespoon dried basil
- ¼ teaspoon ground black pepper
- 1 tablespoon dried oregano
- ¼ teaspoon red pepper flakes
- 1 tablespoon dried sage
- 1 tablespoon dried thyme
- 3 teaspoon coconut sugar
- 1/2 of lemon, juice
- 1/4 cup red wine

Method:

1. Take a large saucepan, place it over medium heat, add tomatoes and remaining ingredients, stir and simmer for 1 hour or more until thickened and cooked.
2. Serve sauce over pasta.

Nutrition Value:

- Calories: 110 Cal
- Fat: 2.5 g
- Carbs: 9 g
- Protein: 2 g
- Fiber: 2 g

Garlic Alfredo Sauce

Preparation time: 10 minutes
Cooking time: 5 minutes
Servings: 4

Ingredients:

- 1 1/2 cups cashews, unsalted, soaked in warm water for 15 minutes
- 6 cloves of garlic, peeled, minced
- 1/2 medium sweet onion, peeled, chopped
- 1 teaspoon salt
- 1/4 cup nutritional yeast
- 1 tablespoon lemon juice
- 2 tablespoons olive oil
- 2 cups almond milk, unsweetened
- 12 ounces fettuccine pasta, cooked, for serving

Method:

1. Take a small saucepan, place it over medium heat, add oil and when hot, add onion and garlic, and cook for 5 minutes until sauté.
2. Meanwhile, drain the cashews, transfer them into a food processor, add remaining ingredients including onion mixture, except for pasta, and pulse for 3 minutes until very smooth.
3. Pour the prepared sauce over pasta, toss until coated and serve.

Nutrition Value:

- Calories: 439 Cal
- Fat: 20 g
- Carbs: 52 g
- Protein: 15 g
- Fiber: 4 g

Cilantro and Parsley Hot Sauce

Preparation time: 5 minutes
Cooking time: 0 minute
Servings: 4

Ingredients:

- 2 cups of parsley and cilantro leaves with stems
- 4 Thai bird chilies, destemmed, deseeded, torn
- 2 teaspoons minced garlic
- 1 teaspoon salt
- 1/4 teaspoon coriander seed, ground
- 1/4 teaspoon ground black pepper
- 1/2 teaspoon cumin seeds, ground
- 3 green cardamom pods, toasted, ground
- 1/2 cup olive oil

Method:

1. Take a spice blender or a food processor, place all the ingredients in it, and process for 5 minutes until the smooth paste comes together.
2. Serve straight away.

Nutrition Value:

- Calories: 130 Cal
- Fat: 14 g
- Carbs: 2 g
- Protein: 1 g
- Fiber: 1 g

Kale and Walnut Pesto

Preparation time: 5 minutes
Cooking time: 10 minutes
Servings: 4

Ingredients:

- 1/2 bunch kale, leaves chop
- 1/2 cup chopped walnuts
- 2 cloves of garlic, peeled
- 1/4 cup nutritional yeast
- ½ of lemon, juiced
- 1/4 cup olive oil
- ¼ teaspoon. ground black pepper
- 1/3 teaspoon. salt

Method:

1. Place a large pot filled with water over medium heat, bring it to boil, then add kale and boil for 5 minutes until tender.
2. Drain kale, then transfer it in a blender, add remaining ingredients and then pulse for 5 minutes until smooth.
3. Serve straight away.

Nutrition Value:

- Calories: 344 Cal
- Fat: 29 g
- Carbs: 16 g
- Protein: 9 g
- Fiber: 6 g

Cashew Yogurt

Preparation time: 12 hours and 5 minutes
Cooking time: 0 minute
Servings: 8

Ingredients:

- 3 probiotic supplements
- 2 2/3 cups cashews, unsalted , soaked in warm water for 15 minutes
- 1/4 teaspoon sea salt
- 4 tablespoon lemon juice
- 1 1/2 cup water

Method:

1. Drain the cashews, add them into the food processor, then add remaining ingredients, except for probiotic supplements, and pulse for 2 minutes until smooth.
2. Tip the mixture in a bowl, add probiotic supplements, stir until mixed, then cover the bowl with a cheesecloth and let it stand for 12 hours in a dark and cool room.
3. Serve straight away.

Nutrition Value:

- Calories: 252 Cal
- Fat: 19.8 g
- Carbs: 14.1 g
- Protein: 8.3 g
- Fiber: 1.5 g

Nacho Cheese Sauce

Preparation time: 15 minutes
Cooking time: 5 minutes
Servings: 12

Ingredients:

- 2 cups cashews, unsalted, soaked in warm water for 15 minutes
- 2 teaspoons salt
- 1/2 cup nutritional yeast
- 1 teaspoon garlic powder
- 1/2 teaspoon smoked paprika
- 1/2 teaspoon red chili powder
- 1 teaspoon onion powder
- 2 teaspoons Sriracha
- 3 tablespoons lemon juice
- 4 cups water, divided

Method:

1. Drain the cashews, transfer them to a food processor, then add remaining ingredients, reserving 3 cups water, and, and pulse for 3 minutes until smooth.
2. Tip the mixture in a saucepan, place it over medium heat and cook for 3 to 5 minutes until the sauce has thickened and bubbling, whisking constantly.
3. When done, taste the sauce to adjust seasoning and then serve.

Nutrition Value:

- Calories: 128 Cal
- Fat: 10 g
- Carbs: 8 g
- Protein: 5 g
- Fiber: 1 g

Thai Peanut Sauce

Preparation time: 10 minutes
Cooking time: 10 minutes
Servings: 4

Ingredients:

- 2 tablespoons ground peanut, and more for topping
- 2 tablespoons Thai red curry paste
- ½ teaspoon salt
- 1 tablespoon sugar
- 1/2 cup creamy peanut butter
- 2 tablespoons apple cider vinegar
- 3/4 cup coconut milk, unsweetened

Method:

1. Take a saucepan, place it over low heat, add all the ingredients, whisk well until combined, and then bring the sauce to simmer.
2. Then remove the pan from heat, top with ground peanuts, and serve.

Nutrition Value:

- Calories: 397 Cal
- Fat: 50 g
- Carbs: 16 g
- Protein: 26 g
- Fiber: 4 g

Garden Pesto

Preparation time: 5 minutes
Cooking time: 0 minute
Servings: 10

Ingredients:

- 1/4 cup pistachios, shelled
- 3/4 cup parsley leaves
- 1 cup cilantro leaves
- ½ teaspoon minced garlic
- 1/4 cup mint leaves
- 1 cup basil leaves
- ¼ teaspoon ground black pepper
- 1/3 teaspoon salt
- 1/2 cup olive oil
- 1 1/2 teaspoons miso
- 2 teaspoons lemon juice

Method:

1. Place all the ingredients in the order in a food processor or blender and then pulse for 3 to 5 minutes at high speed until smooth.
2. Tip the pesto in a bowl and then serve.

Nutrition Value:

- Calories: 111.5 Cal
- Fat: 11.5 g
- Carbs: 2.8 g
- Protein: 1.2 g
- Fiber: 1.4 g

Buffalo Chicken Dip

Preparation time: 5 minutes
Cooking time: 15 minutes
Servings: 4

Ingredients:

- 2 cups cashews
- 2 teaspoons garlic powder
- 1 1/2 teaspoons salt
- 2 teaspoons onion powder
- 3 tablespoons lemon juice
- 1 cup buffalo sauce
- 1 cup of water
- 14-ounce artichoke hearts, packed in water, drained

Method:

1. Switch on the oven, then set it to 375 degrees F and let it preheat.
2. Meanwhile, pour 3 cups of boiling water in a bowl, add cashews and let soak for 5 minutes.
3. Then drain the cashew, transfer them into the blender, pour in water, add lemon juice and all the seasoning and blend until smooth.
4. Add artichokes and buffalo sauce, process until chunky mixture comes together, and then transfer the dip to an ovenproof dish.
5. Bake for 20 minutes and then serve.

Nutrition Value:

- Calories: 100 Cal
- Fat: 100 g
- Carbs: 100 g
- Protein: 100 g
- Fiber: 100 g

Hot Sauce

Preparation time: 10 minutes
Cooking time: 15 minutes
Servings: 6

Ingredients:

- 4 Serrano peppers, destemmed
- 1/2 of medium white onion, chopped
- 1 medium carrot, chopped
- 10 habanero chilies, destemmed
- 6 cloves of garlic, unpeeled
- 2 teaspoons sea salt
- 1 cup apple cider vinegar
- 1/2 teaspoon brown rice syrup
- 1 cup of water

Method:

1. Take a skillet pan, place it medium heat, add garlic, and cook for 15 minutes until roasted, frequently turning garlic, set aside to cool.
2. Meanwhile, take a saucepan, place it over medium-low heat, add remaining ingredients in it, except for salt and syrup, stir and cook for 12 minutes until vegetables are tender.
3. When the garlic has roasted and cooled, peel them and add them to a food processor.
4. Then add cooked saucepan along with remaining ingredients, and pulse for 3 minutes until smooth.
5. Let sauce cool and then serve straight away

Nutrition Value:

- Calories: 137 Cal
- Fat: 0 g
- Carbs: 30 g
- Protein: 4 g
- Fiber: 10 g

Alfredo Sauce

Preparation time: 5 minutes
Cooking time: 0 minute
Servings: 4

Ingredients:

- 1 cup cashews, unsalted, soaked in warm water for 15 minutes
- 1 teaspoon minced garlic
- 1/4 teaspoon ground black pepper
- 1/3 teaspoon salt
- 1/4 cup nutritional yeast
- 2 tablespoons tamari
- 2 tablespoons olive oil
- 4 tablespoons water

Method:

1. Drain the cashews, transfer them into a food processor, add remaining ingredients in it, and pulse for 3 minutes until thick sauce comes together.
2. Serve straight away.

Nutrition Value:

- Calories: 105.7 Cal
- Fat: 5.3 g
- Carbs: 11 g
- Protein: 4.7 g
- Fiber: 2 g

Chapter 10: Drinks

Mango Lassi

Preparation time: 5 minutes
 Cooking time: 0 minute
 Servings: 2

Ingredients:

- 1 ¼ cup mango pulp
- 1 tablespoon coconut sugar
- 1/8 teaspoon salt
- 1/2 teaspoon lemon juice
- 1/4 cup almond milk, unsweetened
- 1/4 cup chilled water
- 1 cup cashew yogurt

Method:

1. Place all the ingredients in the order in a food processor or blender and then pulse for 2 to 3 minutes at high speed until smooth.
2. Pour the lassi into two glasses and then serve.

Nutrition Value:

- Calories: 218 Cal
- Fat: 2 g
- Carbs: 44 g
- Protein: 3 g
- Fiber: 1 g

Chard, Lettuce and Ginger Smoothie

Preparation time: 5 minutes
Cooking time: 0 minute
Servings: 2

Ingredients:

- 10 Chard leaves, chopped
- 1-inch piece of ginger, chopped
- 10 lettuce leaves, chopped
- ½ teaspoon black salt
- 2 pear, chopped
- 2 teaspoons coconut sugar
- ¼ teaspoon ground black pepper
- ¼ teaspoon salt
- 2 tablespoons lemon juice
- 2 cups of water

Method:

1. Place all the ingredients in the order in a food processor or blender and then pulse for 2 to 3 minutes at high speed until smooth.
2. Pour the smoothie into two glasses and then serve.

Nutrition Value:

- Calories: 514 Cal
- Fat: 0 g
- Carbs: 15 g
- Protein: 4 g
- Fiber: 4 g

Green Lemonade

Preparation time: 5 minutes
Cooking time: 0 minute
Servings: 2

Ingredients:

- 10 large stalks of celery, chopped
- 2 medium green apples, cored, peeled, chopped
- 2 medium cucumbers, peeled, chopped
- 2 inches piece of ginger
- 10 stalks of kale, chopped
- 2 cups parsley

Method:
1. Process all the ingredients in the order in a juicer or blender and then strain it into two glasses.
2. Serve straight away.

Nutrition Value:
- Calories: 102.3 Cal
- Fat: 1.1 g
- Carbs: 26.2 g
- Protein: 4.7 g
- Fiber: 8.5 g

Banana Milk

Preparation time: 5 minutes
Cooking time: 0 minute
Servings: 2

Ingredients:

- 2 dates
- 2 medium bananas, peeled
- 1 teaspoon vanilla extract, unsweetened
- 1/2 cup ice
- 2 cups of water

Method:

1. Place all the ingredients in the order in a food processor or blender and then pulse for 2 to 3 minutes at high speed until smooth.
2. Pour the smoothie into two glasses and then serve.

Nutrition Value:

- Calories: 79 Cal
- Fat: 0 g
- Carbs: 19.8 g
- Protein: 0.8 g
- Fiber: 6 g

Strawberry and Hemp Smoothie

Preparation time: 5 minutes
Cooking time: 0 minute
Servings: 2

Ingredients:

- 3 cups fresh strawberries
- 2 tablespoons hemp seeds
- 1/2 teaspoon vanilla extract, unsweetened
- 1/8 teaspoon sea salt
- 2 tablespoons maple syrup
- 1 cup vegan yogurt
- 1 cup almond milk, unsweetened
- 1 cup of ice cubes
- 2 tablespoons hemp protein

Method:

1. Place all the ingredients in the order in a food processor or blender, except for protein powder, and then pulse for 2 to 3 minutes at high speed until smooth.
2. Pour the smoothie into two glasses and then serve.

Nutrition Value:

- Calories: 258 Cal
- Fat: 17 g
- Carbs: 12 g
- Protein: 14 g
- Fiber: 2 g

Pumpkin Spice Frappuccino

Preparation time: 5 minutes
Cooking time: 0 minute
Servings: 2

Ingredients:

- ½ teaspoon ground ginger
- 1/8 teaspoon allspice
- ½ teaspoon ground cinnamon
- 2 tablespoons coconut sugar
- 1/8 teaspoon nutmeg
- ¼ teaspoon ground cloves
- 1 teaspoon vanilla extract, unsweetened
- 2 teaspoons instant coffee
- 2 cups almond milk, unsweetened
- 1 cup of ice cubes

Method:

1. Place all the ingredients in the order in a food processor or blender and then pulse for 2 to 3 minutes at high speed until smooth.
2. Pour the Frappuccino into two glasses and then serve.

Nutrition Value:

- Calories: 90 Cal
- Fat: 6 g
- Carbs: 5 g
- Protein: 2 g
- Fiber: 1 g

Turmeric Lassi

Preparation time: 5 minutes
Cooking time: 0 minute
Servings: 2

Ingredients:

- 1 teaspoon grated ginger
- 1/8 teaspoon ground black pepper
- 1 teaspoon turmeric powder
- 1/8 teaspoon cayenne
- 1 tablespoon coconut sugar
- 1/8 teaspoon salt
- 1 cup vegan yogurt
- 1 cup almond milk

Method:

1. Place all the ingredients in the order in a food processor or blender and then pulse for 2 to 3 minutes at high speed until smooth.
2. Pour the lassi into two glasses and then serve.

Nutrition Value:

- Calories: 128 Cal
- Fat: 3 g
- Carbs: 20 g
- Protein: 3 g
- Fiber: 1 g

Red Beet, Pear and Apple Smoothie

Preparation time: 5 minutes
Cooking time: 0 minute
Servings: 2

Ingredients:

- 1/2 of medium beet, peeled, chopped
- 1 tablespoon chopped cilantro
- 1 orange, juiced
- 1 medium pear, chopped
- 1 medium apple, cored, chopped
- 1/4 teaspoon ground black pepper
- 1/8 teaspoon rock salt
- 1 teaspoon coconut sugar
- 1/4 teaspoons salt
- 1 cup of water

Method:

1. Place all the ingredients in the order in a food processor or blender and then pulse for 2 to 3 minutes at high speed until smooth.
2. Pour the smoothie into two glasses and then serve.

Nutrition Value:

- Calories: 132 Cal
- Fat: 0 g
- Carbs: 34 g
- Protein: 1 g
- Fiber: 5 g

Banana and Protein Smoothie

Preparation time: 5 minutes
Cooking time: 0 minute
Servings: 2

Ingredients:
- 2/3 cup frozen pineapple chunk
- 10 frozen strawberries
- 2 frozen bananas
- 2 scoops protein powder
- 2 teaspoons cocoa powder
- 2 tablespoons maple syrup
- 2 teaspoons vanilla extract, unsweetened
- 2 cups almond milk, unsweetened

Method:
1. Place all the ingredients in the order in a food processor or blender and then pulse for 2 to 3 minutes at high speed until smooth.
2. Pour the smoothie into two glasses and then serve.

Nutrition Value:
- Calories: 272 Cal
- Fat: 3.8 g
- Carbs: 59.4 g
- Protein: 4.3 g
- Fiber: 7.1 g

Hazelnut and Chocolate Milk

Preparation time: 5 minutes
Cooking time: 0 minute
Servings: 2

Ingredients:

- 2 tablespoons cocoa powder
- 4 dates, pitted
- 1 cup hazelnuts
- 3 cups of water

Method:

1. Place all the ingredients in the order in a food processor or blender and then pulse for 2 to 3 minutes at high speed until smooth.
2. Pour the smoothie into two glasses and then serve.

Nutrition Value:

- Calories: 120 Cal
- Fat: 5 g
- Carbs: 19 g
- Protein: 2 g
- Fiber: 1 g

Berry and Yogurt Smoothie

Preparation time: 5 minutes
Cooking time: 0 minute
Servings: 2

Ingredients:

- 2 small bananas
- 3 cups frozen mixed berries
- 1 ½ cup cashew yogurt
- 1/2 teaspoon vanilla extract, unsweetened
- 1/2 cup almond milk, unsweetened

Method:

1. Place all the ingredients in the order in a food processor or blender and then pulse for 2 to 3 minutes at high speed until smooth.
2. Pour the smoothie into two glasses and then serve.

Nutrition Value:

- Calories: 326 Cal
- Fat: 6.5 g
- Carbs: 65.6 g
- Protein: 8 g
- Fiber: 8.4 g

Fruit Infused Water

Preparation time: 5 minutes
Cooking time: 0 minute
Servings: 2

Ingredients:

- 3 strawberries, sliced
- 5 mint leaves
- ½ of orange, sliced
- 2 cups of water

Method:

1. Divide fruits and mint between two glasses, pour in water, stir until just mixed, and then refrigerate for 2 hours.
2. Serve straight away.

Nutrition Value:

- Calories: 5.4 Cal
- Fat: 0.1 g
- Carbs: 1.3 g
- Protein: 0.1 g
- Fiber: 0.4 g

Spiced Buttermilk

Preparation time: 5 minutes
Cooking time: 0 minute
Servings: 2

Ingredients:

- 3/4 teaspoon ground cumin
- 1/4 teaspoon sea salt
- 1/8 teaspoon ground black pepper
- 2 mint leaves
- 1/8 teaspoon lemon juice
- ¼ cup cilantro leaves
- 1 cup of chilled water
- 1 cup vegan yogurt, unsweetened
- Ice as needed

Method:

1. Place all the ingredients in the order in a food processor or blender, except for cilantro and ¼ teaspoon cumin, and then pulse for 2 to 3 minutes at high speed until smooth.
2. Pour the milk into glasses, top with cilantro and cumin, and then serve.

Nutrition Value:

- Calories: 92 Cal
- Fat: 2 g
- Carbs: 5 g
- Protein: 11 g
- Fiber: 0.5 g

Strawberry and Pineapple Smoothie

Preparation time: 5 minutes
Cooking time: 0 minute
Servings: 2

Ingredients:

- 2 cups frozen strawberries
- 2 tablespoons almond butter
- 2 cups chopped pineapple
- 1 ½ cup chilled almond milk, unsweetened

Method:

1. Place all the ingredients in the order in a food processor or blender and then pulse for 2 to 3 minutes at high speed until smooth.
2. Pour the smoothie into two glasses and then serve.

Nutrition Value:

- Calories: 255 Cal
- Fat: 11 g
- Carbs: 39 g
- Protein: 6 g

Conclusion

With more and more people rallying behind the need for a healthy lifestyle, a plant-based diet is fast becoming the newest medium for health enthusiasts seeking a sustainable diet module. there is a Plant Based cookbook which is an easy guide for people who are new to this kind of diet. The Plant Based cookbook helps you filter out the confusion and provides information that is easy to consume, even for someone who is just a beginner. The recipes in the book are the result of exhaustive research and careful planning. The book ensures that each recipe listed is simple and follows a systematic approach to make it easy to follow and cook. With the help of the book, the reader can also pick and choose the ingredients of their choice to plan their meals.

Thank you for buying this book. Now let's start your gourmet journey!

www.ingramcontent.com/pod-product-compliance
Lightning Source LLC
Chambersburg PA
CBHW081400070526
44583CB00020B/2612